M000302254

Truly Free

Lisa Scholze

TRILOGY CHRISTIAN PUBLISHERS

TUSTIN, CA

Trilogy Christian Publishers

A Wholly Owned Subsidary of Trinity Broadcasting Network

2442 Michelle Drive

Tustin, CA 92780

For information, address Trilogy Christian Publishing

Rights Department, 2442 Michelle Drive, Tustin, Ca 92780.

Trilogy Christian Publishing/ TBN and colophon are trademarks of Trinity Broadcasting Network.

For information about special discounts for bulk purchases, please contact Trilogy Christian Publishing.

Manufactured in the United States of America

Trilogy Disclaimer: The views and content expressed in this book are those of the author and may not necessarily reflect the views and doctrine of Trilogy Christian Publishing or the Trinity Broadcasting Network.

Cover image: Photo by Andrew Neel from Pexels

10 9 8 7 6 5 4 3 2 1

Library of Congress Cataloging-in-Publication Data is available.

ISBN 978-1-64088-715-2

ISBN 978-1-64088-716-9 (ebook)

Contents

Introduction

So if the Son sets you free, you are truly free!

—John 8:36 (NLT)

You are *forever* saved and *unconditionally* loved by our Lord Christ Jesus and our heavenly Father! Under the new covenant, which we are now under, all sins were forgiven, once for all time, two thousand years ago when Jesus became our sacrifice on the cross. As saved Christians, we are now the righteousness of Jesus as a free gift from our heavenly Father. He isn't mad at you about anything, or holding any sin against you. As a matter of fact, he is always on *your* side. You are *his* child, he made you, and he is madly in love with you! It is his desire for you to thoroughly enjoy your life, with him, to the abundant, to the full, until it overflows! Just to get started, here are three Bible verses of truth directly from your heavenly Father to you:

I will remember their sins and lawless deeds no more. (Heb. 10:17, NLT)

You are precious and honored in my sight and I love you! (Isa. 43:4, NLT)

I have swept away your sins like a cloud. I have scattered your offenses like the morning mist, oh, return to me, for I have paid the price to set you free!
(Isa. 44:22, NLT)

Talk about heartwarming scripture! These are three of my favorites that I wanted to bring to light, right off the bat.

The writing of this book was a true gift to me, and to you, from our heavenly Father. Its purpose is to free you from all unnecessary guilt, condemnation, and wrong thinking, and to show you the truth of the new covenant that our Savior, Jesus, ushered in when he came down to this planet and saved us. Your heavenly Father loves you perfectly, and in his eyes, you are his perfect child.

So let's turn the page for it is written:

You *shall know* the truth, and the truth shall set you free! (John 8:32, NLT)

Overview

Okay, so this is it in a nutshell. We have a Father in heaven who totally loves us, intimately, and he's not mad at us about anything. He wants all of us, his children, to come running back to him in the sinless state he created us in, before the fall of Adam and Eve.

He made a way for this to happen, in a lavish expression of love, through the perfect new covenant. It replaces the old covenant that has been declared obsolete, where animal sacrifices had to be continually offered to temporarily atone for sins. In this new covenant, he sent his Son, our dear Savior, Jesus, to come down here and die on the cross as a final sacrifice as payment for and to completely remove all sin of the world!

There is nothing that we could ever do to undo this new covenant because Jesus never sinned, and it's about him, not us. Saved Christians become the righteousness of Jesus at the moment of salvation, as a permanent free gift, completely independent of anything we are or are not doing. The ability for you to lose your salvation does not exist because Jesus is your Savior, not you.

Jesus's death on the cross and triumphant resurrection paid the price for you to be totally free from all guilt and condemnation.

At the moment of salvation, the Holy Spirit comes to literally live inside every saved Christian, empowering us to live a life of peace, joy, prosperity, and victory over sin.

As children of our heavenly Father, there never exists a period of time where we are out of fellowship with him. He can never be angry with or be disappointed in us, for he sees us as the perfection of Jesus constantly. He can literally see no sin on us even if we make a mistake. The new covenant specifically tells us in Hebrews 10:17 (NLT), "I will never again remember their sins and lawless deeds." That is what you call the good news!

We have become Jesus's little brothers and sisters, enjoying the same heavenly Father, and he never wants us to be afraid of him in any way! He wants to walk hand in hand with us in an intimate and incredibly loving relationship every single moment of our life!

He *passionately loves you*, child of God. You are his kid, and he will never let you down or let you go! Hallelujah!

PART 1:
You Are Forgiven

LISA SCHOLZE

The Sins of All the World Were Forgiven through Jesus Christ Once and for All Time

In today's churches, do we see any more altars where the blood of animals is offered as a sacrifice for sins? Do we still see that? No, of course not. The blood of the final sacrifice of our Savior, Jesus, on the cross paid for sins completely and finally. We don't go around in churches offering animal sacrifices anymore because:

> When sins *have been forgiven*, there is no need to offer any more sacrifices. (Heb. 10:18, NLT)

"When sins *have been forgiven*," that is in the past tense. That's why we don't offer sacrifices anymore. It's as clear as day right there. All sins were forgiven when the final sacrifice was made two thousand years ago by our dear Savior.

Let's look more at what the Bible says in the book of Hebrews about our forgiveness and the finished work of Jesus. Do you want to know what the will of our heavenly Father is regarding our salvation? Well, it's right here.

> *God's will* was for us to be made holy by the sacrifice of the body of Jesus Christ *once for all time.*
> (Heb. 10:10, NLT)

> With his own blood, not the blood of goats and calves, he entered the most holy place, *once for all time*, and secured our redemption *forever*. (Heb. 9:12, NLT)

Jesus was the perfect sacrifice to take away sin *once for all time*. *All* time, means *all* time. What is time as we know it? Past, present, and future. So the sins of the world—past, present, and future—were taken away, once, for *all* time.

Notice the last line says, "secured our redemption *forever*"! *Jesus* secured your salvation; and what he secured, as *your* Savior, you cannot undo. Your heavenly Father has taken from our hands the ability to lose our salvation. *Once for all time*, our salvation has been *secured forever! That* was our Father's will, and that's exactly what happened.

Let's read more from Hebrews:

> He did not enter heaven to offer himself again and again, like the high priest here on Earth, who enters the most holy place, year after year with the blood of an animal. If that had been necessary, Christ would have had to die again and again ever since the world began. But now, once for all time, he has appeared at the end of the age to remove sin by his own death as a sacrifice. (Heb. 9:25–26, NLT)

Payment for sin and forgiveness happened once. We are already forgiven, so Jesus doesn't have to keep coming back down here, repeatedly dying on the cross, again and again, every time somebody fails. Do we see Jesus coming back down here to keep dying for our sins all over again, every day? Does he keep coming back down here to die on the cross constantly? No, of course not. He did it once, and for all time. He *removed sin,* as a whole, from us by dying on the cross as the final sacrifice.

> Christ was offered once for all time as a sacrifice to *take away the sins* of many people. (Heb. 9:28, NLT)

Thank you, dear Savior Jesus!
Let's read more from Romans:

> God, in his grace, freely makes us right in his sight. He *did this* through Christ Jesus when he freed us from the penalty for our sins. (Rom. 3:24, NLT)

Our heavenly Father has made us right in his sight, freely through our Savior, Jesus. Notice again that in the above verse, "*he did this* through Christ Jesus," is in the past tense. "*He freed us* from the penalty of our sins" is also in the past tense. When did he do this? When were we freed from all penalties? Two thousand years ago, all at one time, through Jesus when he was made the sacrifice for all sin. Let's read on:

> For God presented Jesus as the sacrifice for sin. People are made right with God *when* they believe that Jesus sacrificed his life, shedding his blood. (Rom. 3:25, NLT)

We are *made right* with our heavenly Father *when* we believe in Jesus. At the moment of our salvation, when we accept Jesus as our Savior, we are made right with our heavenly Father forever!

Listen to this powerful, one to memorize, truth:

> There is now *no condemnation* for those who are in Christ Jesus. (Rom. 8:1, NIV)

This is the *good news!* Our heavenly Father loves us, and he sees us as the perfection of our Savior, Jesus. There is right *now*, here on earth, *no* condemnation for us about anything, ever. Jesus took all the condemnation and punishment on himself for all sin, as a whole. Jesus has freed you; the same sin cannot be punished twice. You are completely forgiven for everything past, present, and future; and your heavenly Father loves you intimately. He is not, and never will be, angry with or disappointed in you about anything. He sees you as his perfect child that he made, and you belong to him forever!

My whole point here that I want to drive home is that the subject of sin is simply not an issue anymore for the saved Christian as far as our heavenly Father is concerned. *He wants his children back* in the state of righteousness he created them in before the fall of Adam and Eve.

He wants an intimate, loving relationship with us at all times, where we are completely unafraid to run to him in a happy and joyful way, *enjoying* our life with him. He loves us incredibly, and he wants us to live in a state of no condemnation with him. He accomplished just that with the sacrifice of his Son, our Savior, Jesus.

Thank you, Jesus!

CHAPTER 2

The Old Covenant

In order to have a full revelation of our salvation, it's important to be clear on the truth of the old and new covenants.

The old covenant has been canceled and declared obsolete by our heavenly Father. We are solely under the new covenant, which came into effect when Jesus came down to this planet and saved us by shedding his blood on the cross as the final perfect sacrifice.

The old covenant was given to Moses, based on the Ten Commandments, and many other laws listed in the Old Testament. Man tried to keep these laws, but couldn't, as proven here very simply:

> The strength of sin is the law.
> (1 Cor. 15:56, NLT)

Since the strength of sin is the law, it stirs up man's sinful nature when we try to keep it on our own.

> For whoever keeps the whole law and yet stumbles at just one point is guilty of breaking all of it. (James 2:10, NLT)

Without Jesus, we would all be guilty of breaking every law there is because if you break one, you broke them all.

> No one can ever be made right with God by doing what the law commands. The law simply shows us how sinful we are. (Rom. 3:20, NLT)

Clearly, it is proven in God's Word from the book of Romans that trying to keep the law does not make us right with God. The law was put there to simply show us that we cannot keep it because of our sinful nature, and we need Jesus as our Savior.

Before Jesus came, under the old covenant, man sinned, felt guilty, and then animal sacrifices and sin offerings were needed to be continually offered to make atonement for sin.

This is explained to us in the book of Hebrews:

> The sacrifices under that system were repeated again and again, year after year, but they were

never able to provide perfect cleansing for those who came to worship. If they could have provided perfect cleansing, the sacrifices would have stopped, for the worshipers would have been purified once for all time and their feelings of guilt would have disappeared. But instead those sacrifices actually reminded them of their sins year after year. (Heb. 10:1–3, NLT)

Under the old covenant, the priest stands before the altar, day after day, offering the same sacrifices, again and again, which can never take away sins. (Heb. 10:11, NLT)

However, Jesus comes in to save us from this cycle. Here are his own words as quoted to us in Hebrews:

That is why, when Christ came into the world, he said to God: "You did not want animal sacrifices or sin offerings, but you have given me a body to offer." (Heb. 10:5, NLT)

Therefore, Jesus comes down here to offer his body as the final sacrifice.

He cancels the first covenant in order to put the new covenant into effect. (Heb. 10:9, NLT)

Hallelujah!

The old covenant has been canceled, and the new covenant is now in effect.

CHAPTER 3

The New Covenant

The old covenant is canceled, and the new covenant has been ushered in by Jesus!

Let's read the new covenant as it is recorded for us in the book of Hebrews. Hebrews quotes from the book of Jeremiah, the prophet from whom God spoke through to prophecy his plan of salvation for us.

> This is the new covenant I will make with the people of Israel on that day, says the LORD: I will put my laws in their minds, and I will write them on their hearts. I will be their God, and they will be my people. And they will not need to teach their neighbors, nor will they need to teach their relatives, saying, "You should know the LORD." For everyone, from the least to the greatest, will know me already. And I will forgive their wickedness, and I will never again remember their sins. When God speaks of a "new" covenant, it means

he has made the first one obsolete. It is now out of date and will soon disappear. (Heb. 8:10–13, NLT)

Hallelujah! Thank you, Jesus. The old covenant is now obsolete!

I printed the whole new covenant first for us to read in its entirety, but now let's break it down a little.

> But this is the new covenant I will make with the people of Israel on that day, says the LORD: I will put my laws in their minds, and I will write them on their hearts. (Heb. 8:10, NLT)

Our heavenly Father tells us here that he will instruct us through our minds and our hearts, without the old written set of rules. *He* does all the work leading us and guiding us each day, individually, to live a life of victory over sin. For example, under the old covenant, the law says simply, "Do not steal." However, under the new covenant, being empowered by the Holy Spirit living in us, not only will we not want to steal, but we may be led to give to others at the right place and time. God's will becomes something we desire with our hearts and minds.

I will be their God, and they will be my people. (Heb. 8:10, NLT)

Whatever we need, he will supply. We belong to him, we are his people, and he shall supply all of our needs. He is our heavenly Father, yes, of course; but because he is our God, he is the ultimate Supplier and supplies abundantly!

> And they will not need to teach their neighbors, nor will they need to teach their relatives, saying, "You should know the LORD." For everyone, from the least to the greatest, will know me already. (Heb. 8:11, NLT)

Under this new covenant of complete forgiveness, we live in a constant state of no condemnation with our dear Father. He loves us, his dear children, and we can always be with him, never fearing him. Each of us can now know him in an intimate, loving way without having to be taught by others.

> And I will forgive their wickedness, and *I will never again remember their sins*. When God speaks of a "new" covenant, it means he has made the

first one obsolete. It is now out of date and will soon disappear. (Heb. 8:12–13, NLT)

The last two lines are the main clauses of the new covenant. Our sins *are forgiven* and will *never again* be remembered, and *the old covenant is obsolete.*

Repeated sacrifices of the old covenant are now over. The final sacrifice has been made by our dear Savior, Jesus. When he says, "I will never again remember their sins," the word "remember" means, "he once knew." Your salvation is not contingent upon you knowing your sins and asking for forgiveness. Your salvation is contingent upon the fact that your heavenly Father *already knew all the sins of the world* and punished them on Jesus. All sins—past, present, and future—*were seen* by him and are already forgiven. This is the main point that the new covenant clearly states, "Our sins *are forgiven and will never again be remembered.*"

We as saved Christians have become the righteousness of Jesus with no more sin on us, once for all time. Let's read from the book of John:

Look, the Lamb of God who *takes away the sin of the world.* (John 1:29, NLT)

"The sin of the world" means the sin of the *world*. All sins are *taken away!* Our Lord Jesus took the punishment on himself, in our place, so we could be forgiven forever. The sins of our lifetime—for me, for you, and everyone—of the world have been punished on Jesus at the cross. Two thousand years ago, when Jesus died for us, all of our sins were in the future then, since we weren't even born yet. He took away the "sin" of the world, as a whole, all sin—past, present, and future.

This new covenant is what you call a lavish expression of love that our heavenly Father has for us. He doesn't do anything in some tiny, half-baked way. He does everything big, complete, and abundantly, all powered by him and not by us.

For you see, the old covenant is a big list of don'ts, a big set of rules that are impossible to keep due to man's sinful nature. With the new covenant, everything is freely provided to us by our Father through the sacrifice of Jesus. *He* gives us a clean slate forever. *He* forgave our sins, and *He* promises to never again remember them. *He* leads us in our hearts and minds. *He* provides for us. We just simply believe in Jesus and be saved.

We are now made right with our heavenly Father, just the way he wants it. He wants *you* back with him in a loving and intimate way with the subject of sin no longer being an issue.

The only way to never fear your heavenly Father and be with him constantly in a loving relationship is to know you are completely forgiven for everything—past, present, and future. In this way, we know that there is never any way he could possibly ever be angry with us because all his anger was exhausted at the cross when Jesus was punished for the sins of the world.

Your heavenly Father loves you like crazy, and he promises to never again remember our sins. He saw all the sins of the world at one time and made Jesus the sacrifice as payment for them, the most wonderful loving gift we could ever receive. What sounds too good to be true definitely *is true!* The good news!

Thank you, dear Savior Jesus!

If you want to talk about some comforting scripture, let's read what our heavenly Father tells us in the book of Isaiah:

> I have swept away your sins like a cloud, I have scattered your offenses like the morning mist. *Oh return to me, I have paid the price to set you free!* (Isa. 44:22, NLT)

Amen and amen!

CHAPTER 4

Our Salvation Is a Free Gift

Let's read more of the truth of our free gift of salvation from Romans and Ephesians:

> Because one person disobeyed God, many became sinners. But because one other person obeyed God, *many will be made righteous.* (Rom. 5:19, NLT)

That one person that disobeyed God was Adam, and through him, we all became sinners. The other person who obeyed God was Jesus, by dying on the cross for *our* sins. Jesus, of course, never sinned, and he shed his perfect blood for us as payment for our sins. When we accept him as our Savior, we become his righteousness.

God saved you by his grace when you believed. You cannot take credit for this; it is a gift from God. Salvation is not a reward for the good things we have done, so none of us can boast about it. (Eph. 2:8–9, NLT)

Let's let this really sink into our brains here. *God saved you* by his grace. Salvation is a *gift* from God. It is not a reward for the good things we have done. The Greek word here for "salvation" is "*sozo*," which means to be healed, delivered, restored, and made whole. Hallelujah!

God, in his grace, *freely* makes us right in his sight. He did this through Christ Jesus when he freed us from the penalty for our sins. For God presented Jesus as the sacrifice for sin. People are made right with God when they believe that Jesus sacrificed his life, shedding his blood. (Rom. 3:24–25, NLT)

Freely, God declares that we are righteous when we believe in Jesus! You cannot generate righteousness on your own because you don't have any. The only true righteousness there is, and that counts, is Jesus. Saved Christians are saved forever because our salvation is based on the fact that *Jesus* never sinned. We become *his* righteousness as a free gift.

So in this same light, let's say there's an older man, about ninety years old, completely unsaved his whole life because he has never heard about Jesus. He lived a life on the streets, taking and selling illegal drugs, stealing from and assaulting people, along with a lot of other crimes. Then one day, he was walking down the street past this big church and he heard the preacher inside, so he went in and sat down to listen. He was just *overwhelmed* and believed the truth about Jesus and salvation. So he looked up toward heaven and prayed, "Dear Jesus, I accept you as my Savior. Thank you for saving me!" Right at that instant, he became a saved Christian. Our heavenly Father is rejoicing in heaven with angels! The old guy will now be there with those angels in heaven one day. Since he is now a saved child of God, the Holy Spirit came to literally live inside of his earthly body. He became a new creation, becoming the righteousness of Jesus and has the same righteousness as the pope! There are not different levels of righteousness. Jesus's perfection is Jesus's perfection, and that is the *gift* of righteousness on the saved believer.

On the other hand, there is a guy who gives a million dollars every year to the church, goes to church every Sunday, helps little old ladies cross the street, and volunteers in the soup kitchen once a week, but also completely denies Jesus. He declares that he doesn't need or believe in Jesus at all. He thinks he's a good-enough person on his own and should go to heaven anyway because he's such a great guy doing all this good stuff. Well, unfortunately, unless this guy eventually accepts Jesus as his savior, he will not be saved.

Now of course, giving money to the church and helping little old ladies are great things to do. Saved Christians are led to do these things as fruit of the Holy Spirit all the time. I'm using an extreme here to illustrate that good works do not get a person saved. Only believing in Jesus and receiving *his* righteousness will one be saved. Let's read more from Romans:

> For no one can ever be made right in God's sight by doing what his law commands, the law simply shows us how sinful we are. But now God has shown us a different way of being made right in his sight, not by obeying the law, but by the way promised in the scriptures long ago. We are made right in God's sight when we trust in Jesus Christ to take away our sins. And we all can be saved in the same way, no matter who we are or what we have done. (Rom. 3:20–22, NLT)

Our salvation is not dependent on anything that we are doing. Our salvation was accomplished when Jesus died on the cross for us.

Let's simply rest in the finished work of our Savior, Jesus, who loves you very much. Let's not be worried about good deeds achieving or bad deeds losing your salvation because Jesus's righteousness is your salvation. He is your savior, not you!

Hallelujah and thank you, dear Jesus!

CHAPTER 5

You Have Eternal Right Standing with Our Heavenly Father—He Says So

Back when I was born, I was given the last name Mellott. I was born to my mom and dad, Mary Ann and Roy Mellott. Therefore, it became my inherent right to be called a Mellott. That is my standing no matter what I do or what I don't do. Even though I'm now married, my maiden name is still Mellott. Whether I'm in Pittsburgh or Alaska, whether I eat meat or chicken, whether I steal or don't steal, it does not matter; I remain a Mellott.

In the same way, when we become born again, a saved Christian, we have right standing as the righteousness of Jesus with our heavenly Father forever, completely independent of our actions. He tells us so in his Word from Romans:

Who dares accuse us whom God has chosen for his own? No one—for God himself *has given us right standing with himself.* (Rom. 8:33, NLT)

"*Has given*" is in the past tense. Saved Christians already possess right standing with our heavenly Father. It has been given to us by him. We have been chosen; we belong to our dear Father as his own. Hallelujah! Thank you, dear Savior Jesus!

This next one is the clincher, one of my all-time favorite Bible verses, one to memorize.

You are holy and blameless as you stand before him without a single fault. You must continue to believe this truth and stand in it firmly. (Col. 1:22–23, NLT)

This is definitely the *truth*! Our heavenly Father sees us standing before him *without a single fault.*

We must remember this truth always, especially when we sometimes fail and sin down here, which we may do from time to time. Jesus paid the price for us to have his right standing, no matter what. Our righteousness is not based on what we are or are not doing.

Our right standing with our heavenly father is based on the fact that Jesus never sinned. And we are now *his* righteousness. We don't have any righteousness on our own to generate, keep, or maintain. We are now Jesus's righteousness. We honor him whenever we constantly remember this truth.

> As he is [in heaven], *so are we* here in this world. (1 John 4:17, KJV)

As Jesus is, so are we right *now*, in this world! Right here on this planet. Not only someday when we arrive in heaven, but now our heavenly Father sees us as the perfection of his Son, Jesus. Saved Christians are *now* all his sons and daughters, just as Jesus is his Son.

Is our heavenly Father mad at Jesus about anything? No. He's not mad at us either.

Does he see any sin on Jesus? No. He doesn't see any sin on us either.

Does he love Jesus intimately and lavishly? Yes, of course! And he loves us in the same way intimately and lavishly!

Let's remember from Hebrews and Corinthians that this salvation is forever:

He entered the most holy Place, *once for all time*, and secured our redemption forever. (Heb. 9:12, NLT)

Right standing is *forever*, no matter what we do or don't do!

If anyone is in Christ, he is a new creation. The old has passed away; behold, the new has come. (2 Cor. 5:17, NLT)

Jesus's perfection comes upon us, and we become a new creation, perfect in our heavenly Father's eyes. Forever.

Amen and amen. Thank you, dear Jesus!

CHAPTER 6

Rightly Divide the Word and Know the Truth

The book of Timothy in the Bible is a pastoral letter. Paul writes this letter to young Pastor Timothy to guide him in how and what to teach regarding the good news of Jesus. Paul writes to Timothy:

All scripture is God breathed. (2 Tim. 3:16, NLT)

Therefore, Matthew, Mark, Isaiah, Jeremiah, and everyone else, were the secretaries that penned the Bible to words on paper. They were used to physically write, but the whole Bible is inspired by our heavenly Father. That is why we call it the Word of God.

Paul also teaches that we should correctly explain the Word by:

Rightly dividing the word of truth. (2 Tim. 2:15, KJV)

Therefore, by rightly dividing, we have to know what is being said, and to who. Not all parts of the Bible are intended in a literal sense for the saved Christian. For example, in Deuteronomy, there listed are all the blessings that are meant for the saved Christian. Also listed in Deuteronomy are pages of curses. Those pages of curses are not, literally, to us because we have been redeemed from the curse of the law.

In the same way, I can write a letter to my dear friend Connie. It would say:

Dear Connie,

It's so nice being your friend and meeting with you for coffee every Sunday. I so admire what a wonderful faithful wife you are. Keep up the good work! See you later.

Love,
Lisa

Then I could write another letter to Ms. Homeless Lady. Ms. Homeless Lady is a homeless person who lives on the streets.

Hello Ms. Homeless Lady,

It was nice meeting you the other day. I found out that penicillin might help some of the problems that you're having. We can't go around being so promiscuous all the time. It's not a good way to live. Hope to see you again.

Love,
Lisa

Now I give both letters to Ms. Connie. Both letters are for her to read, learn, and prosper from. However, if she took both letters and just read them, it would seem like I'm contradicting myself to her. The Connie letter is telling her what a wonderful, faithful wife she is. The second letter is about being so promiscuous. However, when we rightly divide the letters, Connie would see that the Homeless Lady letter is not to her in a literal sense. She could read it and learn about penicillin and that there are homeless people around, but she would know that I am not calling her promiscuous, as I was actually writing to the Homeless Lady.

It is the same way with God's Word; he will never contradict himself. Not every part of the Bible is written directly to the saved Christian, but it is all written for us to learn and prosper from. If there is any seeming contradiction, it lies within our interpretation of it.

I want to rightly divide the Word here to explain scripture that many people quote that *seems* very condemning; however, it is *not* intended for the saved child of God. Let's read these next two verses, the first from the book of Matthew and the next from Ephesians:

> But if you refuse to forgive others, your father will not forgive your sins. (Matt. 6:15, NLT)

> Instead, be kind to each other, tenderhearted, forgiving one another, just as God through Christ *has forgiven you*. (Eph. 4:32, NLT)

Obviously, these verses seemingly contradict each other. However, we know our heavenly Father will never contradict himself, and he's not.

The first, the Matthew verse, was quoting Jesus who actually said these words under the old covenant before he even died on the cross, before anyone was saved. He was preaching the law, according to why it was written, to turn people from sin and show they need a savior. For us, this is like the Ms. Homeless Lady letter. It's for us to read and learn from, but it is not written in a literal sense to saved Christians as we are now under the new covenant, saved by our risen Jesus.

The second verse above, the Ephesians verse, is to us. Paul wrote this verse to the young church in Ephesus about thirty years after Jesus died on the cross. It is called a church letter. He wrote to these young Christians, and to us today, to guide them on the truth of their salvation, clearly stating that we have been forgiven. Let's read it again, this church letter that is to us:

> Instead, be kind to each other, tenderhearted, forgiving one another, just as God through Christ *has forgiven you*. (Eph. 4:32, NLT)

Paul also writes to the young church in Colosse, also about thirty years after Jesus died and ascended into heaven. Colossians is another church letter from Paul, and he writes to guide them, and us, in the same way.

> Make allowances for each other's faults, and forgive anyone who offends you. *Remember, the*

Lord forgave you, so you must forgive others. (Col. 3:13, NLT)

All scripture is God-breathed, so the words that Paul writes in the church letters are actually the words of the risen Christ to us, under the new covenant we are now under, with Paul being the secretary inspired by God. He clearly shows us again that we should forgive others since we *have been forgiven.*

Let's rightly divide the Word here again about another verse of scripture that has a lot of Christians believing wrong. Let's read these two verses as recorded both in the book of 1 John.

The first verse, from chapter 1, is *not* written in a literal sense to saved Christians.

> But if we confess our sins to him, he is faithful and just to forgive us our sins and to cleanse us from all wickedness. (1 John 1:9, NLT)

The second verse, from chapter 2, *is* to saved children of God.

> I am writing to you, who are God's children, because your sins have been forgiven through Jesus. (1 John 2:12, NLT)

Now it would seem here again that there is a contradiction between these two verses. However, we know God's Word will not contradict itself. Many people hear the first verse, 1 John 1:9, and think they have to constantly confess sins in order to stay saved, or they need to ask God to keep forgiving them as they go in life. We already know that through all the scripture we have just went over, they prove that this is not the case. However, John was not talking to the saved Christian here. He was addressing false teachers who were claiming that they had no sin to begin with. We must read what John writes before and after this verse in order to see this in its full context:

> We proclaim to you what we ourselves have actually seen and heard so that you may have fellowship *with us*. (1 John 1:3, NLT)

John is talking about having actually seen and heard Jesus. He wants these false teachers to have fellowship with us as saved believers. He wants them to acknowledge they are sinners and accept Jesus.

Let's keep reading:

> But if we are living in the light, as God is in the light, then we have fellowship with each other,

and the blood of Jesus, his Son, *cleanses us from all sin*. If we claim we have no sin, we are only fooling ourselves and not living in the truth. But if we confess our sins to him, he is faithful and just to forgive us our sins and to cleanse us from all wickedness. If we claim we have not sinned, we are calling God a liar and showing that his word has no place in our hearts. (1 John 1:7–10, NLT)

As saved Christians, we are not saying we have not sinned or calling God a liar, of course. John is using the editorial "we" here in talking to these people who claim they have no sin, and he wants them to turn to Jesus. He even goes on to tell these false teachers that the blood of Jesus cleanses us from all sin and cleanses us from all wickedness.

John then starts the second chapter, which *is* written to saved Christians. Let's read again verse 12, which is literally written to us.

I am writing to you who are God's children because your *sins have been forgiven through Jesus*. (1 John 2:12, NLT)

We can clearly see that John tells us, as being saved, dear children of God, that our sins have already been forgiven.

Thank you, Jesus!

LISA SCHOLZE

CHAPTER 7

A Big License to Sin?

Some people ask: will teaching the truth that all of our sins are completely forgiven—past, present, and future—give people a big license to sin?

What?

No.

> My child, don't lose sight of common sense and discernment. (Prov. 3:21, NLT)

Can we really think that our heavenly Father would create a plan of salvation that would cause his children to sin?

Let's remember we have to live completely by the Word. Nowhere in scripture does it state that the new covenant of complete forgiveness will cause his children to sin. In fact, scripture states and proves the exact opposite:

But even greater is God's wonderful grace and his gift of righteousness, for all who receive it will *live in triumph over sin* and death through this one man, Jesus Christ. (Rom. 5:17, NLT)

Therefore, the *truth is* that under the new covenant of grace, we live in triumph over sin through our Savior, Jesus! When we know that our heavenly Father sees us as Jesus's righteousness, and we have been completely forgiven for everything with *never* any condemnation, we can relax and walk hand in hand in love with him every day. We can enjoy his immense love for us, living in peace, joy, and happiness.

Where under the old covenant of the law, there is a big list of don'ts. Don't steal and don't covet, etc. Let's remember:

The law gives sin its power. (1 Cor. 15:56, NLT)

The law simply stirs up the sinful nature of man, giving it power. However, we have been freed from sin and its power, as proven here in Galatians and Romans.

But the scriptures declare that we are all prisoners of sin, so we receive God's promise of freedom only by believing in Jesus Christ. (Gal. 3:22, NLT)

For sin shall no longer be your master, because *you are not under the law, but under grace.* (Rom. 6:14, NLT)

This is one of the most powerful truths of scripture—we are not under the law, but under grace. So since the strength of sin is the law, the way to be free from a life of sin, to have sin not be our master, is to be free from the law, saved through Jesus and under the new covenant of grace. We rest in the finished work of Jesus saving us.

Therefore, as *his* righteousness, the Holy Spirit lives in us, leading us to live a life of victory over sin. For all saved Christians have the Holy Spirit living in them.

The Spirit of God, who raised Jesus from the dead, lives in you. (Rom. 8:11, NLT)

That is amazing, *completely* amazing! The ultimate, powerful Holy Spirit, *who raised Jesus from the dead,* literally lives in us, right inside our physical bodies! Truly contemplating that fact leaves me in awe. That is why we are called the temple of the Lord, and saved Christians can never be possessed by some evil spirit.

The Spirit who lives in you is greater than the spirit who lives in the world. (1 John 4:4, NLT)

When the powerful Holy Spirit is living in you, which he is forever, no evil spirit can get in there. You are protected forever.

The Holy Spirit also *empowers* us constantly to live a life of victory over sin through the nine gifts we have received, as listed in here in Galatians:

But the fruit of the Spirit is love, joy, peace, patience, kindness, goodness, faithfulness, gentleness, and self-control. Against such things there is no law. (Gal. 5:22–23, NIV)

The Holy Spirit produces these wonderful attributes of love within us, as fruit, enabling us to live peacefully and joyfully. When we are filled with the fruit of love, we love our neighbor instead of robbing them. When we are filled with patience and self-control, we're not lashing out with arguing or fighting.

But when you are directed by the Spirit, you are not under obligation to the law of Moses. (Gal. 5:18, NLT)

So that is how under the new covenant, we are no longer under the law. We are led by the Holy Spirit in us, empowering us to live a life of *victory over sin*.

Our gifts that the Holy Spirit always produces in us to live a life of happiness and success, let's look at them again:

- love
- joy
- peace
- patience
- kindness
- goodness
- faithfulness
- gentleness
- self-control

These are all certainly attributes of Jesus, so we can become a new creation in him!

As we walk closely every day with our heavenly Father, as his children, in intimate prayer, with the Almighty Creator of the Universe, how could we not reign in life? We are constantly in his presence, being encircled with his love, blessings, guidance, and the gifts of the Holy Spirit who dwells in us!

We have a wonderful life of victory in our Savior, Jesus!

Hallelujah!

CHAPTER 8

Do We Need to Keep Asking for Forgiveness?

In the light of everything that we just went over, this is still a stumbling block for some Christians, simply because of continued wrong beliefs regarding the new and old covenants.

The answer is no, of course not. *You already are forgiven.* Sin is simply not a subject anymore with our heavenly Father and his saved children. Let's hear what our heavenly Father tells us through Isaiah:

> I—yes, I alone—will blot out your sins for my own sake and will never think of them again. (Isa. 43:25, NLT)

We don't need to ask him to forgive us for some sin when he's already blotted them all out. It doesn't matter what it is. It is impossible for him to even think of them. He just said he will never think of them again. How can we ask him to forgive us for something, when it's impossible for him to think of them? So if you have some sin in your past that's been bothering you with guilt feelings, it is totally unnecessary. No matter how terrible it may seem, it doesn't matter because your heavenly Father cannot see it anymore, and you've been forgiven.

He gave up his Son as the sacrifice to have you back as his saved child in a sinless state! He loves you and sees you as his perfect child.

Let's listen to this enlightening and powerful truth from the church letter of Colossians:

> He *canceled the record of the charges against us* and took it away by nailing it to the cross. (Col. 2:14, NLT)

There is no more record of charges against you. They were nailed to the cross two thousand years ago by your Father in heaven. Therefore, there is no need to ask him to forgive us for a charge against us, when there is no charge against us. He *already says* there is no charge against you because Jesus already died on the cross as payment to have those charges removed forever! This is what you call the true *good news!* Thank you, Jesus our Savior!

Thinking that you have to come to your heavenly Father and ask for forgiveness is trying to combine the old and the new covenants together.

Under the old, *obsolete* covenant, the blood of animals only temporarily atones for sin and must be continually repeated.

However, since we are now under the new covenant, let's read again from Hebrews:

> *I will never again remember their sins.* (Heb. 8:12, NLT)

The perfect, final blood of Jesus completely removes sin forever, and our heavenly Father cannot remember any sin.

Coming to your heavenly Father and asking for forgiveness would be like presenting yourself to him as if you are in a state of unrighteousness. As saved Christians, we become the righteousness of *Jesus forever,* as a free gift, completely independent of what we are or are not doing! We are his righteousness because he never sinned. Let's remember:

God himself has given us *right standing* with himself. (Rom. 8:33, NLT)

The truth will *set you free*. (John 8:32, NLT)

If we make a mistake down here and do anything that's wrong, no, we do not have to ask our Father in heaven for forgiveness because we already are forgiven, as all the scripture we just went over again has proven. Jesus was punished on the cross for every sin ever committed—past, present, and future. *All the blame was put on him for everything.*

Let's listen to this powerful truth from Ephesians, which proves and says it all:

He is so rich in kindness and grace that he purchased our freedom with the blood of his Son and *forgave our sins*. (Eph. 1:7, NLT)

Purchased and *forgave* are in the past tense. We have already been forgiven. Forgiveness was bought and paid for two thousand years ago by our savior Jesus's shed blood.

Therefore, we honor Jesus's suffering and death by not even bringing up the subject of that sin with our heavenly Father, in order to be forgiven, because we already are. Jesus is our Savior, not us. He did all the work for us by his suffering and sacrifice on the cross, and by that we are forgiven, not by any additional daily work down here from us. Our heavenly Father gave up his Son for ALL sin, so we could be free and run to him confidently and boldly as the righteousness of Jesus. He loves us immensely and unconditionally. We can now live in that peace and love. We can talk to him about anything that is troubling us. We can go to him for help if we are in a situation because of something we have done wrong down here, and he will help us and make everything turn out for the good.

> And we know that God causes EVERYTHING to work together for the good of those who love God and are called according to his purpose for them. (Rom. 8:28 NLT, emphasis mine)

Everything means everything.

He created this plan of salvation as a tremendous gift of love, in his kindness and grace, so he could have his children back to him in the sinless state he created them in without any way for us to lose our salvation.

I know it can be a very different way of living for someone who has lived their life constantly thinking they have to ask their heavenly Father for forgiveness.

It is a different but fantastically better and true way of living, the way your heavenly Father wants to live with you. It's a life without fear, doubt, or condemnation in a relaxed, joyful way with him, living in the *truth* of *who you are now*, the righteousness of Jesus!

Now this is not saying that we shouldn't ask for forgiveness with our fellow human beings down here. If we make a mistake and do something wrong against someone else, of course, we need to ask another person for forgiveness. But as far as our heavenly Father goes, *he* can't even remember it. That is the grace that we are living under now because of Jesus. It's called the good news. It's called salvation. Thank you, our dear Savior Jesus!

So laugh and talk with your heavenly Father all the time; he loves it and he *loves you*. His unfailing love is surrounding you constantly. You are his kid, and he thinks you're the best thing since sliced bread! It's simply time to relax and enjoy the benefits of your true forgiveness and love that your Savior paid for you to have! It doesn't matter what you did or didn't do. Run into his presence confidently and joyfully at all times, right into his open and loving arms. You are his child, and he loves you *a ton*, unconditionally.

Always be joyful. Keep on praying. No matter what happens, always be thankful, for this is God's will for you who belong to Christ Jesus. (1 Thess. 5:16–18, NLT)

Joyful. Prayerful. Thankful. Amen!
Thank you, dear Savior Jesus!

CHAPTER 9

Forgiven Much, Love Much

As part of our heavenly Father's loving plan of salvation for us through Jesus, when we know all sin—past, present, and future—has been forgiven completely, it causes us to live a life of love, not sin. It enables us to love him and others *much*.

Let's look at how this truth is recorded for us in the book of Luke. This is a fascinating true account that has a lot of revelation in it for us. Jesus was invited to dinner at the home of a religious leader, a Pharisee, when a sinful woman comes in. Let's read on:

> One of the Pharisees asked Jesus to have dinner with him, so Jesus went to his home and sat down to eat. When a certain immoral woman from that city heard he was eating there, she brought a beautiful alabaster jar filled with ex-

pensive perfume. Then she knelt behind him at his feet, weeping. Her tears fell on his feet, and she wiped them off with her hair. Then she kept kissing his feet and putting perfume on them.

When the Pharisee who had invited him saw this, he said to himself, "If this man were a prophet, he would know what kind of woman is touching him. She's a sinner!"

Then Jesus answered his thoughts. "Simon," he said to the Pharisee, "I have something to say to you."

"Go ahead, Teacher," Simon replied.

Then Jesus told him this story: "A man loaned money to two people—500 pieces of silver to one and 50 pieces to the other. But neither of them could repay him, so he kindly forgave them both, canceling their debts. Who do you suppose loved him more after that?"

Simon answered, "I suppose the one for whom he canceled the larger debt."

"That's right," Jesus said. (Luke 7:36–43, NLT)

I'm going to stop right here for one second. We are like the man who owed the five hundred pieces of silver, not just the fifty-piece guy. *All* of our sins—past, present, and future—have been forgiven, not just a little.

Knowing that *all* of our big debts have been paid causes us to love him, and others, more! Let's keep reading.

> Then he turned to the woman and said to Simon, "Look at this woman kneeling here. When I entered your home, you didn't offer me water to wash the dust from my feet, but she has washed them with her tears and wiped them with her hair. You didn't greet me with a kiss, but from the time I first came in, she has not stopped kissing my feet. You neglected the courtesy of olive oil to anoint my head, but she has anointed my feet with rare perfume." (Luke 7:44–46, NLT)

So this woman, who knew that her sins were forgiven, like us, had an intimate loving relationship with him immediately. She was weeping and kissing him! The Pharisee, the religious leader, could only see the law and sin, and had no revelation of forgiveness or love for Jesus.

> "I tell you, her sins—and they are many—have been forgiven, so she has shown me much love. But a person who is forgiven little shows only little love." Then Jesus said to the woman, "Your sins are forgiven."

The men at the table said among themselves, "Who is this man, that he goes around forgiving sins?"

And Jesus said to the woman, "Your faith has saved you; go in peace." (Luke 7:47–50, NLT)

Here, the religious leaders, representing the law, didn't have a loving relationship at all with Jesus, or even know who he really was.

This woman knew all her sins were forgiven, like us, and loved much. That is part of the wonderful plan of salvation. When we know that we are forgiven much, we don't want to sin more; we love more. We love our heavenly Father and others more, and live in peace. We get to enjoy an intimate, loving relationship with our Father, knowing there will never be any condemnation from him.

What a wonderful teaching! Thank you, Jesus!

PART 2:

You Are Loved

CHAPTER 10

Jesus Already Saved You! Just Say, "Yes!"

Becoming a saved Christian is not complicated at all. All the work has already been done by Jesus.

If you're not sure if you are saved, or you know you're not, and you want to be, you can become a saved Christian right now. You can instantly become the righteousness of Jesus, and the Holy Spirit will literally come to live inside of you at that moment. It doesn't matter what you have done in the past. It was already put on Jesus. Jesus took the punishment and shed his blood as a sacrifice for every single murder, theft, act of adultery—you name it. *All sin ever committed, or will be committed,* was already seen by our Father, and our Savior Jesus was punished for it and it was *forgiven*. Yours were in there, right along with the rest of us. Jesus has you covered. It's already been seen, punished, and forgiven by our heavenly Father. All you have to do is accept this salvation. Jesus saved you. He died on the cross, was laid in the tomb, and on the third day, Resurrection Sunday, God raised him from the dead triumphantly.

It has been made so easy for us to receive this wonderful gift of salvation. Let's read how from the book of Romans:

> If you confess with your mouth that Jesus is Lord, and believe in your heart that God raised him from the dead, you will be saved. (Rom. 10:9, NLT)

That's it. It's that simple.

If you're not a saved Christian yet, and you want to be the righteousness of Jesus, to start living in the kingdom right now, on this earth, and spend eternity in heaven, I invite you to say this prayer with me:

> Dear Heavenly Father,

> Thank you for sending Jesus to save me. I declare with my mouth and receive that Jesus is my Lord and Savior, and he died on the cross for me. His shed blood has paid for all my sins—past, present, and future—and they are forgiven. I believe, heavenly Father, that you raised him from

the dead, and that he is alive right now with you in heaven as my eternal Savior. Thank you, Jesus, for saving me! Amen.

Well, if you just said that prayer with me, you've become a saved Christian! That was the best decision you have ever made. You are now a new creation in Christ Jesus! Your heavenly Father is rejoicing over you with angels, and he *has you back!* You don't have to keep repeating the prayer; you are saved forever. Hallelujah!

You have become the righteousness of Jesus, just now, instantly! The Holy Spirit now lives, literally, *inside of you!* Your heavenly Father loves you *tons*, and he sees you as his perfect child forever. He is proud of you! You are *his* kid, and his immense love is constantly encircling you. He will never leave you or ever be angry with you, but is loving you forever perfectly!

He wants to talk with you all the time, so keep on praying. Talk with him intimately about everything, and pour your heart out to him. He loves you. You're his little creation. He's rejoicing over you and has amazing plans for your life!

I'm so excited for you! Your new life has begun, your amazing new life in Christ. Your heavenly Father is right with you always, taking care of you and leading you, with him. He will always be on *your* side, child of

God. You've just stepped into the kingdom. The kingdom doesn't follow worldly ways. Your heavenly Father is opening doors for you of opportunity and leading you through them. He is blessing you beyond your wildest dreams.

You will never die. Saved Christians simply change locations, going from our earthly bodies right into heaven.

> Yes, we are fully confident, and we would rather be away from these earthly bodies, for then we will be at home with the Lord. (2 Cor. 5:8, NLT)

> For God so loved the world that he gave his one and only Son, that whoever believes in him shall not perish but have eternal life. (John 3:16, NLT)

> No eye has seen, no ear has heard, and no mind has imagined what God has prepared for those who love him. (1 Cor. 2:9, NLT)

Your eternity has already begun. You're living in the kingdom now, then right into heaven.

Here are two more verses to you from your heavenly Father:

You are always with me and all that I have is yours! (Luke 15:31, NIV)

You are precious and honored in my sight, and I love you! (Isa. 43:4, NLT)

Congratulations, kingdom kid, child of God! Hallelujah!

LISA SCHOLZE

CHAPTER 11

Calling Him Abba Father

Our dear Father in heaven actually wants us to call him Daddy.

I know that may sound crazy if you're not familiar with this, but listen to this wonderful truth of his Word for us in the book of Galatians.

> When the right time came, God sent his Son, born of a woman, subject to the law. God sent Him to buy our freedom for us who were slaves to the law, so he could adopt us as his very own children. And because we are his children, God has sent the Spirit of his Son into our hearts, *prompting us to call out "Abba, Father."* Now you are no longer a slave, but God's own child. And since you are his child, God has made you his heir. (Gal. 4:4–7, NLT)

The Spirit of his Son into our hearts, that's the Holy Spirit who lives inside of us. Through his Word here, he is prompting you to call out Abba Father.

The word "Abba" is an Aramaic term that young children use to call their fathers—Daddy, addressing them in a very intimate and loving way. Therefore, in the English language, "Abba" would be translated as "daddy." Similarly, in the French language, it would be "papa."

Paul tells us the same thing again in Romans:

> So you have not received a spirit that makes you fearful slaves. Instead you received God's Spirit when he adopted you as his own children. *Now we call him "Abba, Father."* For his Spirit joins with our spirit to affirm that we are God's children. (Rom. 8:15–16, NLT)

You have a Dad in heaven, the ultimate loving Dad. In this situation, you are the little kid. It doesn't matter how old you are; and your Dad in heaven wants an affectionate, intimate, and loving relationship with you. His Word tells us clearly right here that he wants us to call him Daddy, or Dad, if you're more comfortable with that. The name Dad is just such a personal, loving, and intimate name that he wants to be called, and he clearly tells us here in his Word.

Remember:

> You shall know the truth and the truth shall set you free. (John 8:32, NLT)

Amen!
Hallelujah!
Thanks, Dad!

LISA SCHOLZE

CHAPTER 12

We Are in Loving Awe, Not Fear

I want to clear up any wrong thinking about fearing our heavenly Dad. A lot of people think that we should be "in fear" of God. Well, not on this side of the cross. In order for us to be afraid of him for some reason, he would have to be mad at us for some reason. We already know he's not mad at us about anything because he was mad at Jesus about everything, when Jesus saved us from all of our sins. Now our Dad in heaven sees us as his perfect children, which we are!

Let's read from the book of Psalms a powerful statement:

> But you offer forgiveness, so that we may learn to fear you. (Ps. 130:4, NLT)

The Old Testament was originally written in Hebrew. The original Hebrew meaning for the word "fear" in this psalm is not fright or to be afraid of, but to be in "awe" of, in a loving way. This totally makes this verse clear since the first part talks about how we are offered forgiveness so that we may learn to be in awe of him. We are offered total forgiveness, for all sin—past, present, and future—so we can know that our Dad in heaven can never be angry with us. We now live in awe of him and his love for us.

Let's read more from Psalms.

> The Lord's delight is in those who fear him, those who put their hope in his *unfailing love*. (Ps. 147:11, NLT)

The second half of this sentence, "those who put their hope in his unfailing love," is an adjective phrase describing the first half. Just like in the sentence: I like chocolate cake, a tasty treat. The second half of the sentence, tasty treat, is describing the chocolate cake as an adjective phrase. "Those who put their hope in his unfailing love" is describing those who are in awe of him, certainly not fearing him. Which again puts this sentence in correct context since the word "fear" here, again, means, "in loving awe."

On top of all this, he *delights* in us when we are in loving awe of him, and when we trust in him and his unfailing love for us! Your Dad delights in *you*!

Because of Jesus and forgiveness, there simply is no more reason for fear. Now we can live in love with our Dad in heaven, which is exactly what he wants.

Thank you, Jesus!

LISA SCHOLZE

CHAPTER 13

Nothing Can Separate You from His Intimate Love

Let's listen to this powerful word of truth from the book of Romans:

> And I am convinced that nothing can ever separate us from God's love. Neither death nor life, neither angels nor demons, neither our fears for today, or worries about tomorrow. Not even the powers of hell can separate us from God's love. No power in the sky above or in the earth below, indeed, nothing in all creation will ever be able to separate us from the love of God that is revealed in Christ Jesus our Lord. (Rom. 8:38–39, NLT)

I love that scripture. It is so comforting to read! Nothing *in all creation* will ever be able to separate us from the love of our Dad! That means not even us! We are part of creation; therefore, there's nothing that we could ever do to be separated from him and his love. There is no action that you could take that would stop your heavenly Father from seeing you as the perfection of Jesus, or to stop him from loving you. He loves you unconditionally. Neither our fears for today nor our worries about tomorrow can separate us from his love! So if you have times where you're afraid or worried about something, he is still loving you and blessing you no matter what! There is nothing that exists on this planet that could come in between you and your Dad, or keep his lavish love from pouring out on you.

You are his kid that he made, and his love for you is powerful and personal.

> I made you, and I will care for you. I will carry you along and save you. (Isa. 46:4, NLT)

> See how very much our Father loves us, for he calls us his children, and that is what we are! (1 John 3:1, NLT)

His love that he has for you is an intimate love. He loves each one of his children individually. Just like most parents, I love all my children. I have four—Jessie, Renae, Gregg, and Bob. I love all four, but I love each one of them individually and specifically. Each one is unique in their own ways, and I know and love everything about each one. Can I or anyone else be a better parent than our heavenly Dad? No, of course not. Not even close. He may have billions of kids, but he still loves each and everyone of us individually. He can do that. He is God. Our Dad in heaven, yes, but also the Almighty Creator of the universe. What he creates, he cares for and loves perfectly, and intimately. He tells us so:

> The very hairs on your head are all numbered. (Matt. 10:30, NLT)

I'll say that's pretty intimate. He knows how many hairs are on your head at any given time. Literally.

> The Lord directs the steps of the godly, he delights in *every detail* of their lives. (Ps. 37:23, NLT)

Every. Detail. Your Dad *delights* in you! Every single detail of your life is important to him. He watches over you very carefully and loves you specifically and perfectly. Let's read the psalm that King David wrote, for it's the same for us today.

> You see me when I travel and when I rest at home. You know everything I do. You know what I am going to say even before I say it, Lord. You go before me and follow me. You place your hand of blessing on my head. Such knowledge is too wonderful for me, too great for me to understand! (Ps. 139:3–6, NLT)

Our Dad sees our life up close all the time. If it matters to you, it matters to him. So stay super close with him in prayer. Joyfully, and maybe sometimes tearfully, talk with him about everything going on in your life as your day goes on. He's always keeping his eye on us—at work, at home, on vacation, sleeping or awake. He has you, and his hand of blessing is on you.

So expect your life to always be filled with special favor, opportunities, deals, and perfect timing, with you being in the right place at the right time! You're a kid in the kingdom, and your Dad is watching out for you!

We have a life of victory when the Almighty Creator of the universe, our Dad, is always on our side, and nothing can ever separate us from him and his intimate love!

SO IF THE SON SETS YOU FREE, YOU ARE TRULY FREE!

Amen and amen!

Thanks, Dad!

LISA SCHOLZE

CHAPTER 14

Parable of the Lost Son—Me and You

One of the best examples from the Bible of the love that our Dad in heaven has for us is shown in the Parable of the Lost Son. Jesus himself told the story, and it's recorded for us in the book of Luke. We, of course, are the kids in this story, and the dad is our heavenly Dad. It's fun to read, and it's not that long, so let's get to it:

> A man had two sons. The younger son told his father, "I want my share of your estate now before you die." So his father agreed to divide his wealth between his sons.
>
> A few days later this younger son packed all his belongings and moved to a distant land, and there he wasted all his money in wild living. About the time his money ran out, a great famine swept over the land, and he began to starve.

He persuaded a local farmer to hire him, and the man sent him into his fields to feed the pigs. The young man became so hungry that even the pods he was feeding the pigs looked good to him. But no one gave him anything.

When he finally came to his senses, he said to himself, "At home even the hired servants have enough food to spare, and here I am dying of hunger! I will go home to my father and say, "Father, I have sinned against both heaven and you, and I am no longer worthy of being called your son. Please take me on as a hired servant." (Luke 15:11–19, NLT)

Okay. At this point in our story, this young kid tells his dad he wants his inheritance money even before the dad dies, which his father is kind enough to give. Then after blowing all this money by running around wildly, he finds himself in a famine land and is now literally starving in a pig field. However, he has some wrong thinking going on here. He thinks he has to create this little rehearsed speech, asking to become a servant in the house, so he can literally get some food and live. Let's read on:

So he returned home to his father. And while he was still a long way off, his father saw him coming. Filled with love and compassion, he ran to his son, embraced him, and kissed him. His son said to him, "Father, I have sinned against both heaven and you, and I am no longer worthy of being called your son."

But his father said to the servants, "Quick! Bring the finest robe in the house and put it on him. Get a ring for his finger and sandals for his feet. And kill the calf we have been fattening. We must celebrate with a feast, for this son of mine was dead and has now returned to life. He was lost, but now he is found." So the party began. (Luke 15:20–24, NLT)

His father saw him from a long way off. He was always watching for him. He was filled with love and compassion and ran to the son. Then, there was not one word of condemnation from the father. The dad *never* said *one word* about any of the blown money. Do you notice how the father cut him off in the middle of this rehearsed speech before the kid could even finish? His father wouldn't even let him ask to be taken on as a hired servant. That's because he will never be a servant. He is forever a son!

The first thing the dad does is to tell the real servants to get the finest robe for his son, which is the robe of righteousness. Next, he orders the ring for his finger, which symbolizes authority as a son of the family. Next are the sandals for his feet, for the sons of the family wear sandals and only servants go barefoot. Then he gives the orders for the fattened calf to be killed so he can start a feast and *have a party!* This wonderful father is a wonderful illustration of our wonderful Dad in heaven. He's not mad at us about anything, and he has not even one bit of condemnation for us, ever. He's always watching over us, and providing for us, even having a party, celebrating when his children come back to him! Let's continue with the story:

> Meanwhile, the older son was in the fields working. When he returned home, he heard music and dancing in the house, and he asked one of the servants what was going on. "Your brother is back," he was told, "and your father has killed the fattened calf. We are celebrating because of his safe return."
>
> The older brother was angry and wouldn't go in. His father came out and begged him, but he replied, "All these years I've slaved for you and never once refused to do a single thing you told

me to. And in all that time you never gave me even one young goat for a feast with my friends. Yet when this son of yours comes back after squandering your money on prostitutes, you celebrate by killing the fattened calf!" (Luke 15:25–30, NLT)

This other son had some wrong thinking going on also. He thought he had to be out in the field slaving in order to earn blessings. That was not true because he's actually a son. He also said the father never even gave him one young goat. But back at the beginning of the story, we're told that the dad divided the wealth between his two sons. Let's read on and finish the story:

> His father said to him, "Look, dear son, you have always stayed by me, and everything I have is yours. We had to celebrate this happy day. For your brother was dead and has come back to life! He was lost, but now he is found!" (Luke 15:31–32, NLT)

By simply coming to the father, both sons received exactly what they needed: love, compassion, physical needs abundantly met, and wrong thinking corrected, and all without a word about past mistakes. They are now abundantly provided for and know that they are loved sons forever, no matter what, of their dear loving dad, and never servants.

This is *exactly* what we have with our dear Dad in heaven because in the righteousness of our Savior, Jesus, we are his sons and daughters.

Just like the sons in this story, all we have to do is come to our heavenly Dad if we need anything, or are worried or confused. He's already there, with his arms wide open, throwing his arms around our neck, kissing us, and with never one word of condemnation.

If we have wrong thinking going on or even wrong actions, he doesn't correct us with punishment at all. He corrects us with his word, his love, provision, and wisdom. The first thing he did when his son came back home was order that the robe of righteousness be put on him. So the first thing he did was remind him of his righteousness.

When you know you are the righteousness of God because of Jesus, you live like it.

So the party began! (Luke 15:24, NLT)

Amen and thank you, Jesus!

CHAPTER 15

Assured of His Glad Welcome!

Many years ago, I worked for a big corporation in the chairman of the board and the president's office. This corporate office was on the very top floor of the tall office building, In order to get up there every morning, I went up the regular bank of elevators with everyone else.

Then I would go to a special elevator, where a guard would be sitting all day. He would take a key and ride me up in this special elevator to the corporate office. Once I got up there, it was beautiful, with ornate furniture and expensive paintings everywhere. There was a receptionist desk you had to get by first, then a big long hallway with doorways leading to secretaries' offices. You had to go through the secretary's office in order to get to the chairman or the president's office, and only then if you had an appointment, which was not easy to get. But the funny thing was, whenever the family of one of these top executives came in, they would come right up that elevator without question. They would blow right past the receptionist, the secretaries, and walk right into the private office, into the welcoming arms of their dad, and *rightly so.*

Now in the same way, you know where I'm going here (yes, I'm laughing), we have the same thing right *now.* The big CEO of the universe is *your dad.* At any time, you can run right up to him in prayer, directly into his welcoming arms, no matter what, perfect child. He *loves* it! He loves *you!* You are precious to him, you are his, and you are *royalty*, a kid of the King!

> Because of Christ's faithfulness, we can come fearlessly into God's presence, assured of his glad welcome. (Eph. 3:12, NLT)

Fearlessly into God's presence! *Assured of his glad welcome!* That is music to my ears, and I'm sure to yours too. He's always welcoming us because of Christ's faithfulness in becoming our Savior.

Our Dad in heaven sent us a big sign to prove it! Let's read what happened the moment Jesus gave up his Spirit and died on the cross.

Then Jesus uttered another loud cry and breathed his last, and the curtain in the sanctuary was torn in two from top to bottom. (Mark 15:37–38, NLT)

The curtain in the sanctuary is referring to the curtain in the temple that separated the Holy Place from the Most Holy Place. Only the high priest could enter the Most Holy Place, where God's presence was, and only once a year.

So when Jesus died on the cross, that curtain was torn apart by God himself, showing us we can go right into his presence, assured of his glad welcome, always!

Your Dad in heaven loves you and wants you to come running freely to him at all times!

There is nothing there to stop you. He is always with you. He is always watching over you. You become more aware of his presence when you talk to him. So run right up that special elevator of prayer; you are right in his loving and encircling arms!

Hallelujah and thank you, Jesus!

LISA SCHOLZE

CHAPTER 16

Walk on Vacation Grass Every Day with Your Dad

I was incredibly blessed as a child. I was given a wonderful earthly dad, good ol' Roy Mellott. He was a wonderful Christian and loved my mom, and us four kids, immensely and unconditionally, with never any condemnation about anything. He's in heaven now, but because of him and my mom, good ol' Mary Ann, I had a wonderful childhood.

One of my earliest memories was on vacation with our family in Massachusetts. I must have been about five years old. My mom, dad, my brother, and my sisters packed into the family car and started our trek from Pittsburgh up to Cape Cod. We were on our way to a little village of white cottages that sat right along the beach. Of course, it turned out to be great, and one afternoon, my dad and I were walking along the sidewalks that connected the cottages. I can remember the little yards in front of each one and seeing the white sand all mixed in with the green grass. I thought that was so neat, like vacation grass. Back at home, it was just plain grass. I can clearly remember walking hand in hand as we were strolling along. I looked up at my dad and said, "Isn't it something how it turned out to be so nice up here?"

He looked down at me, smiling, and said, "Yep, that's because we have a Father in heaven, who loves us very much. He's always watching out for us and taking care of us," and he reached down and ruffled my hair. There we went, swinging hands along as we walked, and all was right with my little world. That was basically my life with him all the time. He always told us kids that he would never be mad at us if we ever got into trouble, and to come to him about anything. So not only did I have this great dad here on Earth, but he taught us all about our heavenly Father and how much he loves us. So it's very easy for me to see and know the same love that our Dad in heaven has for all of us.

If you also had a dad like mine, well, that's great. But if you didn't, and you had a dad that wasn't so good or maybe wasn't there at all or even abused you, that has *nothing* to do with your heavenly Father and you. Sometimes, people who didn't have great dads have a hard time envisioning or accepting the fact they have a heavenly Dad who loves them *so* much and will never hurt them in any way. Well, I'm here to tell you that you and I have the same heavenly Father, and *he loves you* a ton and is always on *your* side.

> This I know, God is on my side! [Amen!] (Ps. 56:9, NLT)

> Everyone who believes that Jesus is the Christ has become a child of God. (1 John 5:1, NLT)

Here are some true and loving verses of love from his Word that are directly from your Dad in heaven to you.

> You are precious and honored in my sight and I love you. (Isa. 43:4, NLT)

> Fear not, I have redeemed you; I have summoned you by name; you are mine. (Isa. 43:1, NLT)

That's why it was so important for me at the beginning of this book to go through all that scripture about how forgiven we are and that it's impossible for our Dad to be mad at us about anything. You can rest in the fact that your heavenly Father sees you as perfect, just as Jesus is, that you are *his* child; and he will never leave you or cannot stop loving you. He wants to enjoy your life with you intimately, and walk hand in hand with you along vacation grass every day.

> You are *always* with me, and all that I have is yours. (Luke 15:31, NLT)

Hallelujah and amen!
Thanks, Dad!

CHAPTER 17

Love Notes to You

My child, pay attention to my words, listen carefully to what I say. Don't lose sight of them. Let them penetrate deep within your heart, for they bring life to those who find them, and are healing to their whole body. (Prov. 4:20–22, NLT)

This is exactly what we are going to do here. I'm going to show you words directly from your heavenly Dad to *you*. He just told us to pay attention to his words. Reading and rereading these verses will bring the reality of his love for you right into the forefront of your mind and deep into your heart, bringing you peace and *joy*! Plus, and a big *plus*, like the last line says, reading his Word is actually healing to our bodies!

He says, "Don't lose sight of them!" So I encourage you to go back and read these all the time. Maybe you could even copy your favorite ones on index cards or on your phone notes. Then you could keep them with you for an instant dose of love directly into your heart when you need it throughout the day. Let's remember:

> The Word of God is living and powerful. (Heb. 4:12, NLT)

We have to start this list with my two absolute favorites.

> Fear not I have redeemed you, I have summoned you by name, *you are mine.* (Isa. 43:1, NLT)

> You are precious and honored in my sight and *I love you!* (Isa. 43:4, NLT)

> I will heal you of your faithlessness, and my love will know no bounds, for my anger will be gone forever. (Hos. 14:4, NLT)

> You are altogether beautiful, my love; there is no flaw in you. (Song of Sol. 4:7, NLT)

> Unfailing love surrounds those who trust in the Lord. (Ps. 32:10, NLT)

> This I know, God is on my side! (Ps. 56:9, NLT)

You can be sure of this: the Lord set apart the godly for himself. (Ps. 4:3, NLT)

I know the Lord is always with me. I will not be shaken, for he is right beside me. (Ps. 16:8, NLT)

See how very much our Father loves us, for he calls us his children and that is what we are! (1 John 3:1, NLT)

You will show me the way of life, granting me the joy of your presence, and the pleasures of living with you forever. (Ps. 16:11, NLT)

His unfailing love for us is *powerful*, the Lord's faithfulness endures forever. (Ps. 117:2, NLT)

Be strong and courageous. The Lord your God will be with you wherever you go. (Joshua 1:9, NLT)

I have loved you with an everlasting love, my people. I have drawn you to myself. (Jer. 31:3, NLT)

Surely your goodness and mercy and unfailing love will pursue me, all the days of my life. (Ps. 23:6, NLT)

We, out of all creation, have become his most prized possession. (James 1:18, NLT)

You are always with me, and all that I have is yours. (Luke 15:31, NLT)

God's love has been poured into our hearts, by the Holy Spirit, who has been given to us. (Rom. 5:5, NIV)

Christ will make his home in your hearts, as you trust in him. Your roots will go down into God's love and keep you strong, (Eph. 3:17, NLT)

Fear not, I am with you. (Isa. 41:10, NLT)

May you have the power to understand, as all God's people should, how wide, how long, how high, and how deep his love is. (Eph. 3:18, NLT)

Give thanks to the LORD, for he is good; his faithful love endures forever. (Ps. 107:1, NLT)

Those who look to him for help will be radiant with joy. (Ps. 34:5, NLT)

God is love. (1 John 4:8, NLT)

Remain in my love. (John 15:9, NLT)

I can never escape from your Spirit! I can never get away from your presence! (Ps. 139:7, NLT)

Even if my father and mother abandon me, the Lord will hold me close. (Ps. 27:10, NLT)

The Lord your God is with you. He is mighty to save, he will take great delight in you. He will quiet you with his love, and rejoice over you with singing. (Zeph. 3:17, NLT)

Be sure of this, I am with you always, even to the end of the age. (Matt. 28:20, NLT)

We love you back, Dad!
Amen!

CHAPTER 18

No Sickness Is Ever from Our Heavenly Father

Sickness, financial lack, accidents, or anything negative ever happening in *any* way is never *from* our heavenly Dad.

He loves us incredibly! He never wants to see any of us sick, hurt, or be in need. As his children, we receive only his blessings of provision and healing from him.

> The thief's purpose is to steal and kill and destroy. My purpose is to give them a rich and satisfying life. (John 10:10, NLT)

This is Jesus talking here, and the thief referred to is Satan. Satan is the one that steals, kills, and destroys. Jesus came to give us a rich and satisfying life. He accomplished just that by dying on the cross for us. All punishment, for all law breaking of the whole world, was put on Jesus. This truth is explained to us here in the book of Galatians.

> Christ has rescued us from the curse pronounced by the law. When he was hung on the cross, he took upon himself the curse for our wrongdoing. (Gal. 3:13, NLT)

We are not cursed anymore because Jesus took our curses on him for our wrongdoings!

The prophet Isaiah clearly illustrates what happened when Jesus died for us.

> Yet it was our sicknesses he carried; it was our diseases that weighed him down. And we thought his troubles were a punishment from God, a punishment for his own sins! But he was pierced for our rebellion, crushed for our sins. He was beaten so we could be whole. He was whipped so we could be healed. All of us, like sheep, have strayed away. We have left God's paths to follow our own. Yet the LORD laid on him the sins of us all. (Isa. 53:4–6, NLT)

I went ahead and printed the above passage in its entirety so we could read it through completely first. It reveals what Jesus went through for us and why. Let's go ahead and go through the verses:

> Yet it was our sicknesses he carried; it was our diseases that weighed him down. And we thought his troubles were a punishment from God, a punishment for his own sins! But he was pierced for our rebellion, crushed for our sins. (Isa. 53:4–5, NLT)

It was our sicknesses and diseases he carried. So when Jesus died on the cross, he took on our sicknesses and diseases as punishment for our sins. As our Savior, he literally rescued us from all punishment. Even though he never sinned, he was punished as though he did, in place of us receiving it. Your Dad in heaven loves you immensely and wants you completely healthy. He doesn't want us sick, just like we don't want our own kids to be sick. He sent his Son down here to be our savior and be sick for us, so we can be healthy.

> He was beaten so we could be whole. He was whipped so we could be healed. (Isa. 53:5, NLT)

Let's remember that the word "salvation" is actually "*sozo*," which is defined as to heal, restore, deliver, and make whole. Healing and restoration is ours as part of our salvation.

Whenever we do come down with some sort of sickness or need healing in any way, that sickness is never from our Dad in heaven. Healing is from him and is our inherent right. Jesus was beaten and whipped before he died on the cross so we could be healed and made whole.

> All of us, like sheep, have strayed away. We have left God's paths to follow our own. Yet the LORD laid on him the sins of us all. (Isa. 53:6, NLT)

"Sins of us *all*" clearly means all the sins of all the people. Our Dad did not pick and select some sins of some people, but the sins of us all. All of us, of course, are alive at different years throughout the generations. All sins—past, present, and future—was laid on Jesus. He's a perfect Savior, saving every single one of us for every single one of our wrongdoings.

After reading that, I love to listen to what Jesus says to us in the book of John:

> But be of good cheer, I have overcome the world! (John 16:33, NLT)

Thank you and hallelujah, Hero Savior, Jesus!

Get ready here because this is one of the most comforting and enlightening verses of scripture in all the Bible. Since Jesus took upon him the curses for us, this is what our Dad says to us now:

> "But with everlasting love I will have compassion on you," says the LORD, your Redeemer. "Just as I swore in the time of Noah that I would never again let a flood cover the earth, so now I swear that I will never again be angry and punish you. For the mountains may move and the hills disappear, but even then my faithful love for you will remain. My covenant of blessing will never be broken," says the Lord, who has mercy on you. (Isa. 54:8–10, NLT)

Wow, let that sink right into your heart *forever*. Our Dad in heaven will never be mad and punish us. He just promised it right there in his Word to us. He just said, *"So now I swear, I will never again be angry and punish you."* It is impossible for your heavenly Dad to ever be angry with us about anything, even if we do something wrong. Saved Christians still make mistakes. However, right here, he swears he will never be angry with us or punish us. He can do this because as we just read above.

> But he was pierced for our rebellion, crushed for our sins. (Isa. 53:5, NLT)

Jesus was already punished for that mistake.

> And their sins and lawless deeds I shall remember no more. (Heb. 10:17, NLT)

And our Dad's not remembering it.

That is called the lavish gift of salvation, the *true good news*, poured on us in love from our Dad in heaven, paid for by our Savior, Jesus. Our Dad promises to never be angry and punish us, and to faithfully love us and bless us forever!

Thank you, dear Lord Jesus, for saving us!

Thank you, dear Dad in heaven! We love you right back!

Amen.

PART 3:
You Are Blessed

CHAPTER 19

The Deuteronomy 28 Blessings

In the Bible, chapter 28 of the book of Deuteronomy is divided into two parts. The first is the blessings section, and the second is the curses section. The curses listed are *not* for us, as saved Christians. Let's remember again from the previous chapter:

> Christ has rescued us from the curse pronounced by the law. When he was hung on the cross, he took upon himself the curse for our wrongdoing. (Gal. 3:13, NLT)

Instead of being cursed, our Dad in heaven, who loves us, *promises* to shower us with *blessings*.

My faithful love for you will remain. My covenant of blessing will never be broken. (Isa. 54:10, NLT)

We receive all this favor not because of anything we have done, but as a free gift through our Savior, Jesus, since we are now *his* righteousness.

Blessings chase the righteous. (Prov. 13:21, NLT)

These blessings in Deuteronomy 28 are literally chasing us down as we live in the kingdom!

Let's remember as we read this, especially the first line, "if you fully obey," that *Jesus fully obeyed and kept all the commandments perfectly for us,* something that we could never do. We are now his righteousness because he never sinned.

As he is in heaven, so are we here in this world! (1 John 4:17, NLT)

So let's read on:

If you fully obey the LORD your God and carefully keep all his commands that I am giving you today, the LORD your God will set you high above all the nations of the world. You *will experience* all these blessings if you obey the LORD your God:

Your towns and your fields will be blessed. Your children and your crops will be blessed. The offspring of your herds and flocks will be blessed. Your fruit baskets and breadboards will be blessed. Wherever you go and whatever you do, you will be blessed.

The LORD will conquer your enemies when they attack you. They will attack you from one direction, but they will scatter from you in seven! (Deut. 28:1–7, NLT)

Our communities, our children, our finances, and even our *food* are specially blessed. Whatever we are doing, and wherever we go, we will be prospered with special favor. When any kind of enemy tries to attack us, the Lord will fight *for us*, and these enemies will scatter away.

The LORD will guarantee a blessing on everything you do and will fill your storehouses with grain. The LORD your God will bless you in the land he is giving you. (Deut. 28:8, NLT)

"Will fill your storehouses with grain, is referring to our modern-day bank accounts. Your heavenly Dad does not want you lacking in any way financially!

> If you obey the commands of the LORD your God and walk in his ways, the LORD will establish you as his holy people as he swore he would do. Then all the nations of the world will see that you are a people claimed by the LORD, and they will stand in awe of you.
>
> The LORD will give you prosperity in the land he swore to your ancestors to give you, blessing you with many children, numerous livestock, and abundant crops. The LORD will send rain at the proper time from his rich treasury in the heavens and will bless all the work you do. You will lend to many nations, but you will never need to borrow from them. If you listen to these commands of the LORD your God that I am giving you today, and if you carefully obey them, the LORD will make you the head and not the tail, and you will always be on top and never at the bottom! (Deut. 28:9–13, NLT)

Talk about living in the kingdom! Every single base is hit here. Our heavenly Father does not want us to be lacking in any way, and he promises to make us prosper in *everything*. We will always be on top, never at the bottom, in every aspect of our lives.

All of these blessings are inherently ours as being children of the Most High God, saved forever by our Savior, Lord Jesus!

Your Dad in heaven is showering you with his love and provision!

Say amen!

Amen!

Thank you, dear Jesus!

Blessing Notes for You

In addition to the big Deuteronomy 28 chapter of blessings we just read, I've made a list of more great Bible verses on blessings. Just like the list of love notes we read earlier, you can maybe copy your favorites, ones that speak to you, on note cards or your phone. Then anytime you need a dose of the truth, you have them right with you, and you can keep declaring these blessings over you and your family. Before we get to the list, let's remember:

For we walk by faith, not by sight. (2 Cor. 5:7, NASB)

How do we walk by faith and not by sight? We keep on reading his Word and hearing the truth of what our heavenly Father wants us to know. We focus our thinking on what he tells us and not on temporary circumstances that we may see. His Word is powerful and will overtake our minds and hearts.

> Faith comes by hearing, and by hearing the word of God. (Rom. 10:17, NKJV)

Faith is a gift we already have, and it increases through hearing his Word. He gave his Word to us; it is ours. His Word comforts us and gives us specific faith to get us through times that we need it. It's our Dad talking to us! Now of course, the main point here is to get what he is saying into our hearts and minds. However, I take that one step further. Almost always, when I'm reading the Bible or reading chosen Bible verses, I read softly aloud to actually hear the words. I know that may sound a little crazy, like what's the difference, but it does make a difference! The Word of God, the truth, is spoken out to all creation. When we physically hear it, our hearts and minds absorb the Word better, so I hope you try it too!

Let's get to our list:

> You will feed on the treasures of the nations, and boast in their riches. Instead of shame and dishonor, you will enjoy a double share of honor. You will possess a double portion of prosperity in

your land, and everlasting joy will be yours. (Isa. 61:7, NLT)

This same God who takes care of me, will supply all your needs from his glorious riches, which have been given to us in Christ Jesus. (Phil. 4:19, NLT)

My cup overflows with blessings. Surely your goodness and unfailing love will pursue me all the days of my life, and I will live in the house of the Lord forever. (Ps. 23:5, NLT)

The blessings of the Lord makes a person rich, and he adds no sorrow with it. (Prov. 10:22, NLT)

For they are people blessed by the Lord, and their children too, will be blessed. (Isa. 65:23, NLT)

My faithful love you will remain. My covenant of blessing will never be broken. (Isa. 54:10, NLT)

The Lord is my shepherd. I lack nothing. (Ps. 23:1, NLT)

Grace and peace be yours in abundance through the knowledge of God and of Jesus our Lord. (2 Pet. 1:2, NIV)

You know the generous grace of our Lord Jesus Christ. Though he was rich, yet for your sakes he became poor, so that by his poverty, he could make you rich. (2 Cor. 8:9, NLT)

He fills my life with good things. My youth is renewed like the eagle's! (Ps. 103:5, NLT)

Now all glory to God, who is able, through his mighty power at work within us, to accomplish infinitely more than we might ask or think. (Eph. 3:20, NLT)

Only ask, and I will give you the nations as your inheritance, the whole earth as your possession. (Ps. 2:8, NLT)

The godly are showered with blessings! (Prov. 10:6, NLT)

For you bless the godly, O LORD; you surround them with your shield of love. (Ps. 5:12, NLT)

They will live in prosperity, and their children will inherit the land. (Ps. 25:13, NLT)

The LORD gives his people strength. The LORD blesses them with peace. (Ps. 29:11, NLT)

The faithful love of the LORD never ends! His mercies never cease. His mercies begin afresh each morning. (Lam. 3:22–23, NLT)

He who did not spare his own Son, but gave him up for us all, how will he not also, along with him, freely give us all things? (Rom. 8:32, NLT)

Joyful indeed are those whose God is the LORD. (Ps. 144:15, NLT)

Those who trust in the Lord will lack no good thing. (Ps. 34:10, NLT)

I came that they may have life and have it abundantly! (John 10:10, NLT)

You are blessed forever, child of God!
Hallelujah and thank you, our Savior Jesus!

LISA SCHOLZE

CHAPTER 21

Our Hopes Are Granted

Most of us have special hopes and dreams we have in our hearts, and we think about them and would love to see them come true.

A lot of times, those hopes that we have were *put there* by our heavenly Dad! Just like if somebody has a dream of one day opening a bakery. Well, we were all given special gifts and talents, so if you love baking, that love to bake and desire to open a bakery were put there by your Creator, your Dad in heaven!

> "For I know the plans I have for you," says the LORD. "They are *plans for good* and not for disaster, to *give you* a future and a *hope*. (Jer. 29:11, NLT)

So here we are, wondering if he will make our hopes and dreams come true, and he's the one who put them there! Your Dad in heaven has plans for your life, *good* plans for a future with a hope! He wants you to do what you enjoy, and to enjoy your life with your talents.

What does he further tell us in his Word about these hopes that we have?

> The hopes of the godly will be granted. (Prov. 10:24, NLT)

Right to the point, of course! Our hopes will be granted. We are the godly because we are the righteousness of Jesus, our Savior.

Now maybe my example of opening a bakery isn't your idea of fun. I'm talking about anything that you are hoping for, that you want to happen, like a family member becoming a saved Christian, your kids going to college, your daughter finding the right guy to marry, or going on a *vacation*. What do we do with those hopes? We start by turning them into prayers! Get your heavenly Father involved!

Spend time with your dear Dad in heaven and tell him everything that's on your mind and in your imagination. Tell him about the dreams that you have, about what you want! Let's keep turning to the Word. What does he tell us about our prayers?

> The prayers of a righteous man are *powerful*
> *and effective,* producing wonderful results. (James
> 5:16, NIV)

As saved Christians, we are that righteous man or
woman! You are the righteousness of Jesus; and when
you pray, when you talk with your Dad, you will see
powerful and effective results. Being the righteousness
of Jesus is powerful and effective. When we come to
our heavenly Father, as Jesus is, as his child, there is no
limit. We have to keep hearing the truth of the Word, so
let's listen to what he tells us through Hosea:

> *I am the one* who answers your prayers and
> cares for you. I am like a tree that is always green,
> and all your fruit comes from me. (Hos. 14:8, NLT)

Everything good we receive comes from our Dad in
heaven. He is like a tree that is always green, our never-
ending supply!

Wait, it gets better. Listen to this wonderful Word
from Isaiah.

> For they are people blessed by the Lord, and
> their children too, will be blessed. I will answer
> them before they even call to me, while they are

still talking about their needs, I will go ahead and answer their prayers! (Isa. 65:23–24, NLT)

Oh my gosh, can it get any better than that? We are so blessed and loved that while we are still praying, he's going ahead and answering our prayers! The same thing for our children too!

Thank you, dear Dad in heaven. We love you too!

Before we go over this next scripture about prayer, I want to give you this one to read:

> Come to me with ears wide open. Listen, and you will find life! (Isa. 55:3, NLT)

Get ready. Open your ears and listen because you're going to hear this and find life. Your life is going to change because these words are from your Dad in heaven to *you*.

John records for us Jesus talking to his disciples while he was still on earth. He was saying he was about to leave this world soon and go back to be with our Dad in heaven, and what our prayers would be like after that. Like right now.

> At that time, you won't need to ask me for anything. I tell you the truth, you will ask the Father

directly, and he will grant your request because you use my name. You haven't done this before. Ask, using my name, and you will receive, and you will have abundant joy. (John 16:23, NLT)

Okay, that is amazing. He *will grant* your request because you use *his name! You will receive and have abundant joy!* We have everything we need or want in our Savior Jesus.

When Jesus tells us, "He will grant your request because you use my name," of course, verbally use Jesus's name. But more than that, let's remember what we went over earlier. When Jesus died on the cross for us and the curtain ripped in two, it symbolized the fact that we can all go to our Dad directly because we are the righteousness of Jesus in his final shed blood for us. So when we go to our Dad and talk to him, for and about anything, as his loved and saved children, we *are* going to him in the name of Jesus.

So, dear child of God, in Jesus's name, in your righteousness, go *boldly* to your Dad in heaven and ask and receive! Your Dad in heaven will love it. He loves to bless you in every way.

> You take pleasure in showing us your constant love. (Mic. 7:18, NLT)

By coming to him with your wants and needs, as his child, you honor his Son, our savior Jesus's finished work of salvation for you. Then watch as our heavenly Father takes pleasure in showing us his constant love.

Hallelujah!

Thanks, Dad!

Thank you, Jesus!

CHAPTER 22

Don't Worry about Anything

Your heavenly Dad wants you to live a life in complete freedom, and that includes freedom from worrying. He tells us many times in his Word what to do whenever we find ourselves worrying. Let's start here with what Paul writes in the book of Philippians.

> Don't worry about anything, instead, pray about everything. Tell God what you need, and thank him for all he has done. Then you will experience God's peace, which exceeds anything we can understand. His peace will guard your hearts and minds as you live in Christ Jesus. (Phil. 4:6–7, NLT)

These verses here are liquid gold. They clearly tell us to turn every worry into a prayer. I'm sure we all know that a lot people spend a lot of time worrying. Believe me, I've been there too.

It does not have to be that way *at all*. Our heavenly Dad's Word here is true. He clearly tells us in the above verses that *we will* experience *his* peace beyond what we can even understand, guarding our hearts and *minds*. Oh, thank you, Dad. His peace just simply comes upon us without us even understanding how.

Every single time that I have been worried about something, if I stop and tell our Dad about it, tell him what I need, and thank him for, of course, helping, *I immediately* feel relieved. Especially if it's first thing in the morning, it eliminates a ton of worrying that I might have done all day. Because I know, that morning, I prayed about that thing, and my Dad in heaven is working on it.

Many times, worrying is really us constantly going over a situation again and again, trying to decide which way to go, or think of a way out of a problem. When I talk to our Dad in heaven, I always ask *him* to figure a way out and for *him* to make *his* way happen, and to not let anything mess *his* way up, not even *me*. Every time, I always have his peace overtake me. It relieves that burden of trying to figure a way out, which he already knows anyway!

Listen to this great verse from Psalms:

> Cast your burden on the LORD, and he will sustain you; he will never permit the righteous to be shaken. (Ps. 55:22, NIV)

He doesn't want us to be burdened by anything. That's why he *tells* us to cast our burdens on him. *He* will *never* permit us to be shaken. So let's make sure we keep on casting! When we talk to him, let's say, "Here, Dad, I'm throwing this problem to you!" He'll take it. He always does. In fact, he already has it.

We can never have too much of our Dad's words in us. Let's read on:

> When they call on me, I will answer; I'll be with them in trouble. I will rescue and honor them. (Ps. 91:15, NLT)

Never stop calling on your Dad. Lean heavily on him. He will *never* let you down. He tells us right here he will always answer, and he will always rescue us! He's in charge of the whole universe that he made. What seeming problems could we have with this truth in our life? None.

> So let us come boldly to the throne of our gracious God. There we will receive his mercy, and

we will find grace to help us when we need it most. (Heb. 4:16, NLT)

The throne of grace, think of it as running up to your Dad sitting in his big chair because that's exactly what is happening! Our dear Dad wants us to live a life free from anxiety, letting him take care of everything. So let's do just that by staying in the Word, reading these comforting verses, and always coming *boldly* to our dear Dad in prayer. It's there that we will for sure find his grace and mercy to help us with whatever we need.

Let's finish this chapter with my all-time favorite:

Call on *me* in the day of trouble, and *I shall deliver you*. (Ps. 50:15, NLT)

Right to the point. Thanks, Dad in heaven! Amen.

CHAPTER 23

The Battle Is the Lord's

Our Dad in heaven wants to fight our battles for us. He does not want us struggling with earthly battles. Through him, we have already won. "The Lord helps those who help themselves" is not in the Bible. This is what is in the Bible.

King Jehoshaphat was faced with mighty armies about to attack against the people of Judah and Jerusalem. The king did not know what to do, so he said this prayer to our heavenly Dad:

> We are powerless against this mighty army that is about to attack us. We do not know what to do, but we are looking to you for help. (2 Chron. 20:12, NLT)

Here was his answer, which as God's children, is also to us:

> This is what the Lord says, "Do not be afraid of this great multitude, for the battle is not yours, but God's." (2 Chron. 20:15, NLT)

It sure was his battle. Our heavenly Dad made the three big armies that were getting ready to attack Judah and Jerusalem fight against *each other*, killing each other. King Jehoshaphat never even got attacked. His enemies killed each other right before him!

As saved children of the Most High God, the same is true for us today. We already have the victory in every situation we may find ourselves in. That's why our heavenly Dad doesn't want us struggling about what we already have the victory in, but to let him handle it. So whatever battle you may find yourself faced with in life, whether it be a mountain of debt, an illness, someone at your workplace trying to give you trouble, or even a regular old legal battle, call on your Dad in heaven and he will rescue you.

Let's read more from this powerful Word from Isaiah:

Don't be afraid, for I am with you. Don't be discouraged, for I am your God. I will strengthen you and help you. I will hold you up with my victorious right hand. See, all your angry enemies lie there, confused and humiliated. Anyone who opposes you will die and come to nothing. You will look in vain for those who tried to conquer you. *Those who attack you will come to nothing.* For I hold you by your right hand—I, the LORD your God. And I say to you, "Don't be afraid. I am here to help you." (Isa. 41:10–13, NLT)

Talk about amazing scripture. Anyone who attacks us will come *to nothing*. He will strengthen us and confuse our enemies. We are his kids, and he's holding us by the hand and is saying don't be afraid!

Let's keep reading!

The Lord hears his people when they call to him for help. He rescues them from all their troubles. The Lord is close to the brokenhearted; he rescues those whose spirits are crushed. The righteous person faces many troubles, but the Lord comes to the rescue each time! (Ps. 34:17–19, NLT)

He hears us constantly, and he's close to us always. Every single time we need help, our Dad in heaven is running to the rescue!

Let's read a couple more from good old Isaiah:

> But the LORD says, "The captives of warriors will be released, and the plunder of tyrants will be retrieved. For I will fight those who fight you, and I will save your children!" (Isa. 49:25, NLT)

That is so *powerful*. His Word is truly alive. Keep reading it, and those words jump right off the page.

> Whoever attacks you will go down in defeat. (Isa. 54:15, NLT)

We are clearly called to lead a life of rest and let the Lord fight our battles. That does not always mean complete inactivity. If he wants us to do anything, he will guide us, such as what to say to a coworker, or even which lawyer to hire, if need be, but to do it in rest, letting him guide us by peace. However, if he wants us to actually do nothing, he will guide us on that too.

The LORD says, "I will guide you along the best pathway for your life. I will advise you and watch over you." (Ps. 32:8, NLT)

Our Dad is constantly watching over you. You are his dear little child, no matter how old you are down here. He loves you intensely, forever, and he will never let you down about anything.

We already have the victory over any seeming battle!

The horse is made ready for the day of battle, but the victory rests with the Lord. (Prov. 21:31, NLT)

But thanks be to God, he gives us the victory through our Lord Christ Jesus. (1 Cor. 15:57, NIV)

We already have the victory.
Thank you, Jesus, and thank you, Dad in heaven!
Amen!

CHAPTER 24

We Are Protected

As children of the Most High God, living in the kingdom, our families and we are supernaturally protected from harm. His Word tells us so, *a ton*. It's comforting and relieving to meditate on these truths and live in peace. Our Dad in heaven loves us, and he's looking out for us all the time. He even has angels around, protecting and caring for us. Let's read on:

> All who listen to me will live in peace, untroubled by fear of harm. (Prov. 1:33, NLT)

> Every word of God proves true. He is a shield to all who come to him for protection. (Prov. 30:5, NLT)

Let's listen to his true Word and live in peace! As saved Christians, we are not of this world; we are of the kingdom. In this kingdom, there is a shield of protection around us. There are times when we are protected, and we don't even realize it! There is no need for us to walk around fearful.

This next one is a wonderful passage from the book of Psalms. I read it all the time for peace and declare it over my children constantly.

> I look up to the mountains—
> does my help come from there?
> My help comes from the LORD,
> who made heaven and earth!
>
> He will not let you stumble;
> the one who watches over you will not slumber.
> Indeed, he who watches over Israel
> never slumbers or sleeps.
>
> The LORD himself watches over you!
> The LORD stands beside you as your protective shade.
> The sun will not harm you by day,
> nor the moon at night.
>
> The LORD keeps you from all harm
> and watches over your life.

> The LORD keeps watch over you as you come and go,
>> both now and forever.
>> (Ps. 121, NLT)

How comforting is that? Our Dad in heaven is constantly watching over us, protecting us from harm. He never slumbers or sleeps but watches over his children, always, as we come and go, forever. All help ultimately comes from our Father.

Next, we're going to read probably a most well-known promise of protection from the Bible. It's Psalm 91, which covers all the bases! It's sometimes referred to as the prayer of protection. We should read it frequently and declare it over our families and loved ones.

Let's read on:

> Those who live in the secret place of the Most High will find rest in the shadow of the Almighty.
>> This I declare about the LORD:
>> He alone is my refuge, my place of safety;
>> he is my God, and I trust him.
>> For he will rescue you from every trap
>> and protect you from deadly disease.
>> He will cover you with his feathers.
>> He will shelter you with his wings.

His faithful promises are your armor and
protection.
Do not be afraid of the terrors of the night,
nor the arrow that flies in the day.
Do not dread the disease that stalks in
darkness,
nor the disaster that strikes at midday.
Though a thousand fall at your side,
though ten thousand are dying around you,
these evils will not touch you.
(Ps. 91:1–7, NLT)

He shelters us and rescues us from all kinds of attacks and diseases. When you see negative things happening in the world, or reports in the news, they won't
be happening to you or your family. They are the thousand ones falling at your side, and ten thousand around
you.

Just open your eyes,
and see how the wicked are punished.
If you make the LORD your refuge,
if you make the Most High your shelter,
no evil will conquer you;
no plague will come near your home.
For he will order his angels

to protect you wherever you go.
They will hold you up with their hands
so you won't even hurt your foot on a stone.
(Ps. 91:8–12, NLT)

This is the angel part! His Word is true, and we *do* have angels in our presence all the time. An amazing thought, I know, but clearly true!

You will trample upon lions and cobras;
you will crush fierce lions and serpents under your feet!

The LORD says, "I will rescue those who love me.
I will protect those who trust in my name.
When they call on me, I will answer;
will be with them in trouble.
I will rescue and honor them.
I will reward them with a long life
and give them my salvation."
(Ps. 91:13–16, NLT)

When we call on him, he answers! He's our Dad, the Creator of the universe. He will never let us down.

Hallelujah and amen!

CHAPTER 25

Protection Notes for You

Stay in the Word, and you will keep a strong revelation of how protected you are by your heavenly Dad. His Word will overtake you and will let you live in peace, enjoying your life by resting in his strong, sure protection for you and your loved ones.

Let's read first from the prophet Isaiah:

> The rain and snow come down from the heavens and stay on the ground to water the earth. They cause the grain to grow, producing seed for the farmer and bread for the hungry. It is the same with my word. I send it out, and it always produces fruit. It will accomplish all I want it to, and it will prosper everywhere I send it. You will live in joy and peace. (Isa. 55:10–11, NLT)

Our Father's Word produces results! It is like a seed. His Word is alive and will always produce fruit in your life. I've gathered a list of protection verses for you. Just like the love and blessing notes, you could copy down your favorites on notecards or on your phone and read them during the day, declaring them over you and your loved ones. They will give you peace whenever you need it!

Let's read on:

> They will fight you, but they will fail. For I am with you, and I will take care of you. I, the LORD, have spoken! (Jer. 1:19, NLT)

> Fear of man will prove to be a snare, but whoever trusts in the LORD is kept safe. (Ps. 29:25, NLT)

> If God is for us, who can be against us? (Rom. 8:31, NLT)

> The Lord himself will fight for you, just stay calm. (Exod. 14:14, NLT)

This next passage is from the book of Daniel. It was written after Daniel was prevented from being attacked by lions in the lion's den.

> For he is the living God, and he will endure forever. His kingdom will never be destroyed, and his rule will never end. He rescues and saves his people; he performs miraculous signs and wonders in the heavens and on earth. He has rescued Daniel from the power of the lions. (Dan. 6:26–27, NLT)

He will do the same for us today! Miraculous signs. It may not be actual lions, but he will protect us from danger. His rule will never end.

> But in that coming day no weapon turned against you will succeed. You will silence every voice raised up to accuse you. These benefits are enjoyed by the servants of the Lord; their vindication will come from me. I, the Lord, have spoken! (Isa. 54:17, NLT)

> Those who trust in the LORD are as secure as Mount Zion; they will not be defeated but will endure forever. Just as the mountains surround Je-

rusalem, so the LORD surrounds his people, both now and forever. (Ps. 125:1–2, NLT)

He is my loving ally and my fortress, my tower of safety, my rescuer. He is my shield, and I take refuge in him. (Ps. 144:2, NLT)

For he stands beside the needy, ready to save them from those who condemn them. (Ps. 109:31, NLT)

Your godliness will lead you forward, and the glory of the Lord will protect you from behind. (Isa. 58:8, NLT)

God's way is perfect. All the Lord's promises prove true. He is a shield for all who look to him for protection. (Ps. 18:30, NLT)

The LORD frees the prisoners. The LORD opens the eyes of the blind. The LORD lifts up those who are weighed down. The LORD loves the godly. (Prov. 146:7–8, NLT)

Those who look to him for help will be radiant with joy! (Ps. 34:5, NLT)

He reached down from heaven and rescued me; he drew me out of deep waters. He rescued me from my powerful enemies, from those who hated me and were too strong for me. They attacked me at a moment when I was in distress, but the LORD supported me. He led me to a place of safety; he rescued me because he delights in me. (Ps. 18:16–19, NLT)

You are my flock, the sheep of my pasture. (Ezek. 34:31, NLT)

Don't put your confidence in powerful people; there is no help for you there. When they breathe their last, they return to the earth, and all their plans die with them. But joyful are those who have the God of Israel as their helper, whose hope is in the LORD their God. (Ps. 146:3–5, NLT)

In his unfailing love, my God will stand with me. He will let me look down in triumph on all my enemies. (Ps. 59:10, NLT)

Hallelujah, and thank you, dear Jesus!

LISA SCHOLZE

CHAPTER 26

Crazy Thoughts? Who Cares? We Have the Mind of Christ

It is imperative that we stay rooted in the fact that we are the righteousness of Jesus, and all sins have been forgiven—past, present, and future. It is the main truth of the new covenant we are under. If not, unnecessary guilt can set in and try to steal our joy and peace.

Therefore, one of the biggest battles that can take place is inside of our heads, with our thoughts. However, there need not be a battle when we know that our heavenly Dad sees us as perfect no matter what is, or is not, going on in our head.

We can hear the craziest things in our minds. For example, like hearing God's name with swear words, seeing pictures in our imagination of us doing things that we shouldn't be doing, or hearing that we are worthless and will never amount to anything. For someone who doesn't realize the truth, that our Dad in heaven sees us as perfect in Christ, it can be an endless cycle. One of hearing or seeing these things and feeling guilty, depressed, and focusing needlessly on it, even asking for forgiveness, which we all know is totally unnecessary.

Years ago, I used to hear all kinds of crazy things in my head. I would feel guilty unnecessarily because once I learned the truth through his Word that our Dad in heaven sees us as perfect no matter what, all those thoughts just faded away. We are spotless in his eyes, and that's all we need. So what else matters? Sometimes, I still hear craziness, like everyone from time to time, but I could care less. It's just like mind graffiti, a passing thought, that has nothing to do with what we believe, or who we are, or our sound minds.

We have to live by the Word. So let's read on:

> For God did not give us a spirit of fear, but of power, and of love, and of a sound mind. (2 Tim. 1:7, NLT)

The truth of the matter is that we have the Holy Spirit living in us; and we are filled with power and love, not fear, and we have sound minds. Our Dad just said so. That is the truth; anything else *is a lie.*

Furthermore:

We have the mind of Christ. (1 Cor. 2:16, NLT)

That is how our heavenly Dad sees us, as having the mind of Christ, so we have the mind of Christ. It just can't get any better than that!

Dear child of God, your heavenly Dad sees you as perfect no matter what passing thoughts are passing through your head. He loves you. You're not the righteousness of you; you're the righteousness of Jesus.

One of my favorite verses is from the story we read about the lost son who returned home to his Dad.

Focus that sound mind on this:

So the party began! (Luke 15:24, NLT)

He sees you as having the mind of Christ, which you do! Let every day be a party, with you and your Dad!

Amen!

Thank you, Jesus!

LISA SCHOLZE

CHAPTER 27

Ask Big

He who did not spare His own Son, but delivered Him up for us all, how will He not also *with him freely give us all things?* (Rom. 8:32, NASB)

The truth is told to us here in the book of Romans that it is through Jesus we are freely given *all* things. Our heavenly Father gave up his own Son for us so we could be forgiven completely and become his perfection. Jesus is the greatest, most wonderful gift of all, and anything else we could possibly ask for is way under him, no matter how big it *may seem* to us. It's still under him, not even in the same league.

My love will know no bounds! (Hos. 14:4, NLT)

There are no limits in the kingdom in which we live. Earthly ways are not for us. Your heavenly Dad loves you so much he gave you his only Son so that he can bless you with anything.

Don't worry about having enough faith for receiving a big request in prayer. It is not your faith in receiving the request. It's your faith in Jesus being your Savior and the fact that you are now his righteousness, and through *him*, your heavenly Father will bless you with anything. Let's remember what we just read above:

> Will he not also with him freely give us *all things*. (Rom. 8:32, NASB)

> As God hath dealt to every man the measure of faith. (Rom. 12:3, KJV)

We do have faith. It's a gift from our Father, and it's already been given to us. It is the faith that Jesus is our Savior, and that's all we need. Let's read more of the truth of what our heavenly Father tells us from his Word, from the books of John and Mark:

> This is the only work God wants from you: Believe in the one he has sent. (John 6:29, NLT)

> For all things are possible for those who believe. (Mark 9:23, NLT)

All things are possible for those who believe, and we do believe! We do believe in Jesus as our Savior and that we belong to him. That's *all* our heavenly Dad wants from us—to believe in his Son, Jesus, as our Savior, and we do!

Go right ahead. Talk to your Dad in heaven and ask *big*. Ask with no bounds! You honor his Son's sacrifice for you when you boldly come to him and ask for anything. Go ahead and ask for big things in your life because you have a *really big* sacrifice, our Jesus, so you could *do* this. You have a really big Dad in heaven, who has a huge love for you and loves to bless his children abundantly!

It may seem *to us* that what we are asking for is really huge, but it's really not. Because a *huge* overpayment was made, Jesus's life. Take a look at the universe, our Dad's handiwork, and see what he can do. Anything.

If you haven't been, it's time to start talking to your Dad in heaven and *asking big*. Ask in a big way as his child in Jesus and receive in a big way. What's on your mind and heart for you and your family? What are some *big* needs or wants? Don't let anyone tell you that you shouldn't be asking for this or that. All things is all things. Make it a personal request between you and your Dad in heaven. Talk to him intimately. Pour out your heart to him about everything. He loves it, just as he loves you. You're his kid and he's your Dad, and he has the final say. Remember:

> You are always with me, and all that I have is yours. (Luke 15:31, NLT)

Hallelujah, Jesus!
Thanks, Dad!

In Closing

Well, it's been an amazing time here with you. As I said at the beginning, this book has been a gift to me, and to you, from our Dad so you will know the truth, that the Son has set you free! Our Savior Jesus has freed you from all condemnation, fear, lack, worry, and stress so you can live in peace and happiness with your heavenly Dad, as his perfect child, every day. Always focus on the truth of who you are in Christ, and that's his righteousness! Keep meditating on all your favorite scriptures that give you peace and joy!

Your heavenly Dad loves you like crazy and sees you as Jesus's perfection. Nothing you could ever do will ever change that. You are his child forever, and you are his most prized possession. He will always be on your side! He loves to be with you intimately, and he rejoices over you. Stay super tight with him in prayer, every single day. Best time is first in the morning to set your day right. He is always with you, watching over you.

There's a place you can be with him, called the secret place. It's a special place where it's just you and your Dad. You can talk with him intimately in prayer about anything, and he absolutely loves it. You'll be so close with him, closer than the air that you breathe. His loving presence will overtake you and fill you with happiness. Tell him about your problems, hopes, needs, and dreams, everything that's on your mind. He will take care and say yes to it all, in Jesus's name. You are his delight.

> He that dwells in the *secret place* of the Most High shall abide under the shadow of the Almighty. (Ps. 91:1, NLT)

You'll be in that secret place with your Dad, and at the same time, under the shadow of the Almighty Creator of the universe, keeping you safe.

It's there, in that special time with your Dad, in the secret place, that you can ask him for anything; and you will receive it. Let's remember what Jesus says to us as quoted in the book of John:

> I tell you the truth, you will ask the Father directly, and he will grant your request because you use my name. You haven't done this before. Ask,

using my name, and you will receive, and you will have abundant joy. (John 16:23–24, NLT)

That request includes miracles. Because that's what your Dad in heaven is in the business of doing—miracles for you, his kid.

I saved these last two scriptures for last, and they are amazing. They are for you, my dear child of God, so get ready because this is the truth for you.

Yes, says the Lord, *"I will do mighty miracles for you*, like those I did when I rescued you from slavery in Egypt." (Mic. 7:15, NLT)

He *will do* miracles for you! Our Dad just told us he will.

And what was a mighty miracle he did? When the Israelites were standing there on the beach, trapped because if they went backward, they would drown in the ocean; and if they went forward, the Egyptian army was coming ready to kill them as warriors. So what did our Dad do? He created a path through the ocean. He made a wall of water on each side, and his people walked through on dry sand. After they went through safely, the water rushed back in and killed the enemy Egyptians.

If you don't see a way out of some supposed problem, and you need a mighty miracle, your heavenly Dad will make a way you never even dreamed of. And then:

> All the world *will stand amazed* at what *I will* do for you! (Mic. 7:16, NLT)

Oh, my goodness. What else can I say to that?

Get ready. *For amazement. For miracles!* Miracles for you!

Thank you, Dad. Thank you, dear Jesus! We love you back.

Xoxo. Amen.

Stay in his Word, always know that you have a Dad in heaven, and he will *never* leave you nor let you down about *anything*. You are his child. He loves you more than anything in all creation, and you belong to him forever! Walk every day on that vacation grass with him, holding hands. He's reaching down, ruffling your hair.

> So the party began! (Luke 15:24, NLT)

Until next time.

Love, Lisa

Xoxo

CPSIA information can be obtained
at www.ICGtesting.com
Printed in the USA
LVHW081630280120
644893LV00012B/123